Tov

an

Honest

DC Moore's plays for the theatre include *Alaska* (Royal Court Theatre Upstairs, 2007, which won the inaugural Tom Erhardt Award for promising new playwrights) and *The Empire* (Royal Court Theatre and Drum Theatre Plymouth, 2010). His monologue *Honest* was performed at The Mailcoach pub, Northampton, in March 2010. He was also previously an Assistant Director at the Royal & Derngate, Northampton.

DC Moore

Town

and

Honest

Methuen Drama

Published by Methuen Drama 2010

1 3 5 7 9 10 8 6 4 2

Methuen Drama
A & C Black Publishers Limited
36 Soho Square
London W1D 3QY
www.methuendrama.com

ISBN 978 1 408 13301 9

A CIP catalogue record for this title is available from
the British Library

Typeset by MPS Limited, A Macmillan Company
Printed and bound in Great Britain by
Good News Press Limited, Ongar, Essex

Town

Town was first performed at the Royal & Derngate, Northampton, on 18 June 2010. The cast was as follows:

Eleanor	Karen Archer
Anna	Joanna Horton
Mary	Natalie Klamar
Alan	Fred Pearson
John	Mark Rice-Oxley
Ian/Thomas	Tom Robertson

Director	Esther Richardson
Designer	Dawn Allsopp
Lighting Designer	Mark Dymock
Sound Designer	Adam McCready
Movement	Imogen Knight

Characters

Alan
Anna
Eleanor
Ian
John
Mary
Thomas

*'So here I am homeless at home and half gratified
to feel that I can be happy anywhere.'*

John Clare (1841)

Part One

One

Music – 'Inertia' by Jega.

Epping Forest, late summer.

Enter **John,** *walking. Exhausted, lost. He stops, turns, looks the way he's come, before taking in the space around him. He walks towards a clearing and a large tree at the centre of it. But he turns and the forest changes, evaporates. He sees Vauxhall Bridge, London.* **Thomas,** *wearing a suit, calmly climbing up on to the side of the bridge, looking at* **John,** *mouthing something and then stepping from the bridge.*

John *moves towards where* **Thomas** *was but finds himself back in the forest lost, alone.*

Two

A living room in a semi-detached house in Duston, Northampton. Monday afternoon. **Alan** *reads The Daily Telegraph, feet up on a footrest. A pint of bitter in front of him.*

Alan's *mobile receives a text. He reads it. Laughs. Goes back to his paper.*

We hear the front door of the house open.

Alan Y'alright?

No response.

We hear someone go into another room of the house.

After a while, **John** *enters, eating a cheese sandwich he's just made in the kitchen (a slice of bread wrapped around some cheese). He hovers in the door-way.*

Alan You got a plate?

John *shakes his head.*

Pause.

Alan   How was it?

John   Fine.

Alan   Ya legible?

John *nods.*

Alan   How much?

John   Sixty pound, something.

Alan   A month?

John   No, a week.

Alan   Well that's alright. Beer money.

John   Yeah.

Alan   Good stuff.

Alan *nods.*

John *nods.*

Pause.

John   I'm gonna go and read for a bit.

Alan   Here's one for ya.

John   . . . ?

Alan   Pakistani girl.

John   Dad.

Alan   This Pakistani girl, comes to Northampton.

John   Right.

Alan   Within a week, she's fluent.

John   . . . ?

Alan In Polish.

John That's actually.

Alan Good, innit?

John Sort of, yeah.

Alan 'Nother one. Read that.

Alan *picks up his mobile, hands it to* **John***.*

John *reads it.*

John Jesus Christ.

Alan Dunno who thinks 'em up.

John No. Someone.

Alan Yeah.

John Somewhere.

A brief pause.

John *hands the phone back.*

Alan There's more.

John Yeah. Where's Mum?

Alan Shops.

John OK. (*A brief pause.*) She been out all day?

Alan Yeah.

John Right. You want another drink or anything?

Alan Biscuit.

John *exits.*

John (*off*) Figs rolls or fruit shortcake?

Alan Fruit.

John (*off*) Loads or a few?

Alan   Few. On a plate.

After a pause, **John** *enters with the plate of biscuits and also a pint of orange squash he's made for himself. Gives the plate to* **Alan**.

Alan   You taking it off?

John   What?

Alan   Ya coat. You're either going out or coming in.

No response.

John   Town's worse.

Alan   Oh yeah, all the Koskians.

John   Only shop that isn't awful now, is Waterstones.

Alan   Somalis.

John   And that's a bit.

Alan   They're all so fat.

John   What, Somalis?

Alan   No, all the girls.

John   What girls?

Alan   All the girls in town. You see 'em. With their bums hanging out. Bellies. Tattoos. Dunno how they stand it.

John   Who?

Alan   All the boys. Horrible. You sweat a lot, that fat.

John   Yeah. You do.

John *drinks.*

Pause.

Alan   So you alright now then?

John   What?

Alan   F'money?

John Should be.

Alan Just ask, you need any.

John OK.

The door goes again.

Alan Mum.

John Yeah.

Eleanor (*off*) You alright?

Alan In here.

Eleanor (*off*) Only me.

Enter **Eleanor**.

Eleanor How'd it go?

John Not bad.

Alan Sixty pound he's getting.

Eleanor A month?

Alan Don't be stupid woman, a week.

Eleanor *I'm asking my son*. Sixty pounds a week?

John Yeah.

Eleanor Well that'll do.

John *nods.*

Eleanor Tide you over. Keep ya . . . Keep ya going. Won't it?

John Hopefully.

Eleanor Well you can start buying a new pair o' shoes.

John Mum, there's nothing wrong with . . .

Eleanor *You can literally see through them, John.*

John They're . . . comfortable.

Eleanor   You shouldn't be able to see through shoes.

John   No, what about flip flops?

Eleanor   They make you look like a. Bloody. Homeless.

John   Well I am. Sort of.

Alan   He can borrow mine.

Eleanor   He's not gonna wear them, is he?

Alan   They're alright, do me.

Eleanor   Well they won't do him.

John   I'm . . . Alright. I'll get some new shoes.

Eleanor   You should. Good.

A brief pause.

And you need more jeans.

John   Right.

Eleanor   For starters. I mean all your tops are looking a bit.

John   Mum.

Eleanor   Ropey.

John   I really don't need . . .

Eleanor   It's alright, I'll take ya.

John   No, I'll manage.

Eleanor   Drive you down this week. Tomorrow.

John   Mum, I can fucking . . . buy clothes, alright?

Eleanor   Oh. Can you?

Alan   El.

Eleanor   Really?

John   Yeah, I'm . . . Yes.

Alan   Ellie.

Eleanor   Well. 'Manage.' He wouldn't have any clothes if we hadn't driven down there for him. Picked 'em all up.

John   I know.

Eleanor   Would he?

Alan   Eleanor.

Eleanor   He'd a' spent the last month stark naked.

John   OK. Alright. We'll go shopping. This week. Later, this week.

Eleanor   I should think so. And what you got your coat on for? Out tonight?

John   No.

Eleanor   No.

Pause.

Eleanor   So you wanting dinner?

John   Yeah.

Eleanor   Right.

John   What is it?

Eleanor   Shepherd's Pie.

John   Great.

Eleanor   Now come on, you can help me get the shop in. Before the skies open up. Put those muscles to use.

Eleanor *exits.*

Pause.

John   Actually, could I . . . ? Dad, could I . . . ? Borrow a tenner? Till it clears.

Alan *reaches to his wallet, takes out a twenty.*

John   I only need ten.

Alan *holds it out.*

John *takes it.*

John   Shall I take your plate?

Alan *nods and hands it to him.*

John *exits.*

Alan *goes back to the paper. Sips his bitter.*

Three

Later that night. **Anna**'s *bedroom.* **Anna** *and* **John**. *They sit on her single bed. Watching television, drinking red wine from glass tumblers.* **Anna** *is wearing a hooded top; the hood is up. They look at the television as much as they look at each other.*

Anna   Surprise.

John   Yeah.

Anna   Bit of a . . .

John   Imagine.

Anna   How long you back for?

John   Don't know.

Anna   OK. Well. Surprise. Surprise surprise. Cilla Black.

John   Yeah.

Anna   Bob Carolgees. Whole lorra . . . You should have called, or. I could have made some food.

John   Lost my mobile.

Anna   E-mail. Carrier pigeon.

John   I was just walking around and. Saw your light on, thought I'd knock. That's all. I can go, if.

Anna   Yeah no. Ignore me. Just been a long time, that's all.

John   Yeah. (*Pause.*) Your mum and dad look well.

Anna (*genuine question*) Do they?

A long silence, but for the television. They drink.

Anna   You know the most difficult thing about interplanetary space travel?

John   Um. Funding?

Anna   Yeah probably, now. But no, after that.

John *shrugs.*

Anna   Humans.

John   Right. What?

Anna   It's just really fucking difficult. To decide. Who to take. Because it takes like six years or whatever to get to Mars or wherever and back and you can't have more than about ten people in total because of supplies and stuff. But then it's like. Do you have all couples, all single, what? Gay? Do you have an even number for – *sex* – but if you do and you need to vote on anything it'll be like a stalemate. You need at least two doctors, in case one dies. Engineers. Mechanics. Do you have a leader, is it democratic? All this. Like. Do you let them drink? You have to balance them being totally bored and de-motivated against them doing something. *Horrendous.* Yeah, you have to find well-balanced people, with loads of different technical skills *and* the ability to remain sexually fulfilled for ages. Literally like years and years and.

John   Difficult.

Anna   Yeah. Like Blind Date but much much harder. They did this test – the Russians – in the Artic. They got these soldiers to try it for like six months this guy went mental and raped two of the women.

John   Fuck.

Anna   Yeah. Suppose that's what happens when you lock people up in a confined space together, with alcohol, for a long time.

They drink.

Anna   How long have we known each other?

John   Eighteen years.

Anna   Yeah. Better watch your back.

John   OK.

They watch television. Drink.

John   What's he doing now?

Anna   Who?

John   Him. Baldy.

Anna   Patrick Stewart?

John   Yeah.

Anna   He's trying to communicate, with the alien.

John   Which is, difficult?

Anna   Yes.

John   Why?

Anna   It's actually a very good episode.

They drink.

John   I'm probably gonna be back here. Home. For a little while.

Anna   OK. A little little or a lot little?

John   Don't know. Sorted out Jobseekers today.

Anna   How much is that, now?

John   Sixty-five pounds.

Anna   A week?

John *nods. Smiles.*

John   Yeah.

Anna   What? You laughing at me?

John   No. Not at all.

A brief pause.

Anna   So what happened? Down in?

John   What?

Anna   London. Heard you had an OK job with some insurance company. Did they fire you, or . . . ? What happened? You walk out? Have one of your . . . Incredible Hulk moments?

No response.

Anna   No. So what kind of job are you gonna. Seek?

John   Dunno.

Anna   Back to Homebase?

John   Yeah, fuck off.

Anna   Come on, you looked great in green.

John   I really didn't. I don't know. What I'm gonna do.

Anna   I'd say come and work with me but it's complete balls.

John   Most things are.

Anna   Yeah.

John   Like this wine.

Anna   I wasn't gonna say anything.

John   Sorry, it was two for a fiver.

Anna   That's alright, I've had worse.

John   Really?

Anna   No. It tastes like actual bumholes.

They drink.

John   How's your sister?

Anna   Erm yeah. She's breeding. Like a Catholic.

John   Really?

Anna   Just popped out her third.

John   Fuck. That was quick.

Anna   Yeah. Simon, Caryl and now James.

John   Wow. You jealous?

Anna   What?

John   Are you jealous? I . . . just . . . Whenever I see people our age with kids, I get a bit.

Anna   OK.

John   Don't know how they do it.

Anna   By spunking in each other.

John   Well. Yeah.

A brief pause.

John   What's he doing now?

Anna   Failing to make a fire.

John   But the alien can?

Anna *nods.*

Pause.

John   Have I annoyed you?

Anna *shakes her head.*

John   Sure?

Anna *nods.*

Pause.

John   Is there any food?

Anna   Doritos. And some dip. Salsa.

John   Fucking brilliant.

Anna   Yeah. I'll get it in a bit.

John   Thank you.

They drink. Watch television for a while.

John   You wanna hear a joke?

Anna   Go on.

John   It's a little bit. Racist.

Anna   One of your Dad's?

John   Yeah.

Anna   OK then.

John   Alright. Brace yourself.

Four

Later that week. Thursday afternoon. Duston School. **John** *and* **Mary**, *in the playground.*

Mary   Are you a teacher?

John   Me?

Mary   Yeah.

John   No.

Mary   You sure? Coz you look like one. Like one of those scruffy ones. All you need is the beard.

John   OK.

Mary   Yeah.

John *nods.*

Pause.

John   What subject?

Mary   What?

John   I don't – teach – but if I did. What would I? Teach?

She considers.

Mary   Economics.

John   Close.

Mary   Maths?

John   No.

Mary   History.

John   Yeah. That's what my degree was in, anyway.

Mary   OK.

John   Yeah.

Mary   So what you doing here?

John   What?

Mary   Coz if you ain't a teacher, you're just a man in a playground looking at children.

John   Um. Yeah. Mr Stephens was . . . We were just gonna have a quick chat in his office but some kid with a funny little froggy face got punched in the head. He told me to wait here, while he sorted it out.

Mary   So what you're just watching the world go by?

John   Yeah.

Mary   I saw you, from the quadrant.

John   Did you?

Mary *nods.*

Mary   And you was also watching all the girls go by.
I saw you.

John   I wasn't. I've just been . . . Waiting. So. Are you . . . ?
Are you a teaching assistant then, or . . . ?

Mary   *No.*

John   You're a student?

Mary   Yeah.

John   Sorry, I'm terrible with ages, I can't.

Mary   S'alright. Compliment. Yeah.

Pause.

John   I went here. To school.

Mary   What, back in the Eighties?

John   No.

Mary   Seventies?

John   *No.* Nineties.

Mary   Really?

John   Yeah.

Mary   So is it weird being back? You look a little bit
freaked out.

John   I am, a bit.

Mary   And why you meeting Mr Stephens? Are you gonna
help him find a mistress?

John   Don't think so.

Mary   So why you here then?

John   Sorry am I being. Interrogated?

Mary   Only if you've done something wrong.

John   I'm . . . I'm just gonna volunteer to help out. If
Mr Stephens needs any. I've got some spare time, so. You

are now actually making me feel like I've done something wrong.

Mary   Have you though?

John   What?

Mary   Done something?

John   Not today at least, no.

Mary *nods.*

A brief pause.

Mary   When you say you're volunteering, does that mean you won't get paid?

John *nods.*

Mary   So, you've come to hang round your old school for free?

John   Yes.

Mary   Are you sure you're not a paedo?

John   . . .

John *caves in a little and lets out a small laugh/smile.*

John   Yeah, I'm sure, thank you.

Mary *inspects him.*

Pause.

Mary   So shouldn't you have like a proper job?

John   Probably.

Mary   But you don't?

John   No. I'm on. Benefits.

Mary   How much do they pay you for that?

John   Er. Sixty-five pounds and forty-five pence.

Mary   What, a day?

John   No, a week.

Mary *pulls a face.*

Mary   I get paid more than that and I work part-time on the bakery at Sainsbury's. Though I do work Sundays. Overtime.

John   Look, erm. It's lovely to meet you and I don't wanna be rude or anything.

Mary   Then don't be.

John   I'm just waiting for Mr Stephens. He'll be back in a minute.

Mary   So?

John   Well . . .

Mary   What's your name?

John   What?

Mary   What is your name?

John   John.

Mary   John. I'm Mary.

John   OK.

Mary   But you can call me Mary.

John   . . .

Pause.

Mary   Are you clever, John?

John   No.

Mary   You are. I can tell.

John   Alright, yeah, I'm a genius.

Mary   And do you work out?

John   What?

Mary   Coz I think you should. I think you might look alright then.

John   I do.

Mary   *No*.

John   Yes.

Mary   Like what?

John   Running. Swimming. When I can.

Mary   You can't tell. I used to do cross-country. But I gave it up.

Mary *nods*.

John   OK.

Mary   It was rubbish. You just run around. (*Pause*.) So did you see any girls you liked? Whilst you was waiting?

John   No.

Mary   Yeah yeah you did.

John   I didn't.

Mary   It's alright, she can be in Sixth Form. Like me.

John   No, she can't, because I didn't . . .

Mary   You are such a *liar*.

John   . . .

Mary   Aren't you? Unless you prefer boys.

John   . . .

Mary   It's alright, you're welcome to them. Here, they're such. Boys.

John   Yeah, this is getting a bit . . .

Mary   What?

John   Odd.

Mary   Is it?

John   Yeah.

Mary   OK.

A very long pause during which **Mary** *looks around the playground a little.*

Mary   Would you help me?

John   What?

Mary   Would you help me?

John   With . . . ?

Mary   My UCAS. Personal Statement.

John   You're applying? For uni?

Mary   Why, is that . . . . ? Yeah. Are you surprised by that?

John   No.

Mary   So. Will you help me?

John   Erm. OK.

Mary   Why?

John   Because. You asked.

Mary   OK. (*Pause.*) You know what?

John   What?

Mary   You cannot lie.

John   . . .

Mary   Like I saw you. Looking.

Pause.

John   Yeah but only Sixth Form, alright? The uniform thing is actually quite useful.

Mary   What if it's mufti-day for some years?

John   Is it?

Mary   No. But it could have been. Your face.

Five

The next day. Friday, around midday. The living room. **Alan** *is sat reading The Daily Telegraph, drinking bitter.* **John** *is sat reading the Guardian, drinking a pint of orange squash. They read their papers more than they look directly at each other.*

Alan   We can't fight wars no more.

John   No.

Alan   Coz to win you need to be horrible. Be hard, murderous, bastards.

John   Yeah.

Alan   And we can't do it no more, with all the media. All the.

John *nods.*

Alan   Coz the Moslems, they respect force. Arabs. Love it. That's what Saddam was. All he was. Powerful. Tough. Why they miss him.

John   Yeah an Iraqi girl once told me that, in a pub.

Alan   And when you don't know who the enemy are. How can you fight 'em? You can't. (*Pause.*) I like 'em.

John   Who?

Alan   The Moslems. Steal summat, cut off your hands. Know where you are.

John   Right.

Alan   Not like our lot.

John   No. Yeah.

Alan   Cameron. Osborne. What a pair of twats.

John   Yeah. Where's Mum?

Alan   Blair was the worst.

John   She's been out a lot recently. Mornings.

Alan   Brown. Prescott. The size of him. Having affairs.

John   Where does she go?

Alan   Mandelson.

John   Dad.

Alan   Poof. Corrupt. They all are.

John   Dad. Mum.

Alan   Yeah.

John   Where is she?

Alan   Visiting. Elizabeth.

John   Not every day?

Alan   Yeah.

John   Right. What does she . . . do there?

Alan   No idea. And you didn't hear it from me.

John   OK.

A long pause. Back to their papers.

Alan   State of this country. Though we messed the rest of it up as well. Palestine. Africa. Kashmir. We drew the lines. All over. So it's our fault. Innit?

John *looks up from his paper.* **Alan** *continues to read.*

Alan   Yeah.

Six

The following day. Saturday afternoon. Upton housing development. **John** *and* **Anna**, *walking around.* **Anna** *is wearing the same hooded top; the hood is down. We can hear the hum of a near-by motorway.*

John   Fucking hell.

Anna   Yeah.

John   I can literally remember when this was all fields.

Anna   My favorite bit is the earthworks, over there. They've dug holes – pointless holes – and then they've built little bridges over them. It's like. I don't get it. Just leave it as flat ground or.

John   Makes no sense.

Anna   And I'm not sure if it's funny or not but you notice that someone has clearly gone 'Isn't it awful when these new housing estates all look the same?' So what they've done here. Is build nearly every house, in a different fucking style.

John   Yeah.

Anna   I think that's mock-Georgian, where we came up. Then there's sort of warehouse-flat-New-York-loft-bullshit in the middle. Down there by the playing field there's eco-Scandinavian-over-priced-moss-on-the-roof . . . solar . . . cunts. It's mental. It's actually. Mental. We are standing on the product of a diseased mind.

John   Yeah.

Anna   But this is the best bit.

Anna *points to a sign, in the middle distance.*

Anna   So, here we've got the bit that looks all Barratt-homey, little bit chavvy. And it's called. It's actually called

'The Elysian Fields'. See it? That sign? By that kid in the
Rooney shirt.

John *nods*.

Anna   What a world.

John   You're the only person I know who gets genuine
pleasure from badly-designed housing estates.

Anna   Well if that's wrong, I don't wanna be right.
I mean . . . There's an attempt, on one of the other signs,
to capture the philosophy of the estate.

John   Wow.

Anna   *I know*. And there's this bit that says – without any
irony – that 'this is the future of living'. Upton. This . . .
And I've got a horrible feeling that they're completely and
utterly fucking right. The whole world is run by immensely
confident, gaping arseholes.

John   Beautiful. How did you find this?

Anna   Just. Walking around.

John   Really?

Anna *nods*.

Anna   Do it a lot. Walk about. Think.

John   What about?

Anna *shrugs*.

A brief pause.

John   Used to walk around London a lot.

Anna   Yeah?

John   Yeah. Think.

Anna   What about?

John *shrugs*.

John   Biscuits.

Anna   Right.

John   You bought anyone else here?

Anna   No.

John *nods.*

Pause.

Anna   Are we gonna . . .

John   . . . ?

Anna   . . . mention it? Ever.

John   What?

Anna   My sister's. Wedding.

John   Not unless you . . .

Anna   No?

John   No.

Anna   We're just gonna . . .

John   Yeah.

Anna   OK. We don't even wanna . . . ?

John   I don't see . . .

Anna   OK.

John   . . . why

Anna   Course. Water under the.

John   Yeah.

Anna *nods.*

Pause.

John   So where next?

Anna   Er. Maybe. That way?

John   Great.

Anna   I missed you.

No response.

A very long pause.

Quiet. Here.

John *nods.*

Anna   Just the motorway.

They listen to the motorway.

Can hear it from my bedroom. Sometimes leave my window open just to . . . Something about it.

She listens.

Like a song you can't quite make out the words to.

She looks at him.

Pause.

Come on then. Let's go.

Seven

The following Monday. Afternoon. The living room. **Mary** *stands, looking around. A bag on her shoulder.*

Mary   S'alright.

John *(off)*   What is?

Mary   This.

Pause.

John *comes in with a pint of orange squash. Drinks from it.*

Mary   Do I get one?

John   Shit.

John *exits.*

Mary   I don't like orange. Ribena. Blackcurrant. Or Vimto.

Pause.

John *returns with a blackcurrant Ribena. Hands it to* **Mary**.

John   Sorry.

Mary *shrugs.*

John   Not used to visitors.

Mary   This your parents'?

John *nods.*

Mary   They together?

John   Nearly forty years.

Mary   God.

John   Yeah.

Mary   Must be love.

John   Maybe.

Mary   Na, must.

John   I'm just here till I sort out my own place. Temporary. So have you started?

Mary   What?

John   Your statement? UCAS.

Mary   Yeah but it makes me sound a bit. Retarded.

John   I'm sure it doesn't.

Mary *takes the statement, which is neatly pressed inside an A4 exercise book, out of her bag. Hands it to* **John**.

A pause as **John** *reads it.*

Mary See what I mean?

John Hold up.

Pause.

John *has finished, he looks at* **Mary**.

John Yeah, it's not. Great.

Mary But I didn't get no teacher help or nothing.

John You asked?

Mary *nods.*

John Me too.

Mary What, you're applying?

John No, when I was your age. I wanted to go to Oxford or Cambridge and I went to one of the senior teachers – forgotten his name – and he just said 'Er. Right.'

Mary Did he?

John And wished me luck with it. That was it.

Mary So what happened?

John Got an interview.

Mary Where?

John Oxford.

Mary What was it like?

John It was the first time I realised that I wasn't all that clever. I was sat, waiting for the interview. And the guy next to me was talking about how his teacher – obviously from some ridiculously posh school – had given him a reading list over two years, to prepare him. Just for that one interview. And I realised. That I was . . . totally out of my . . .

Mary You are clever though.

John *shakes his head.*

John We got on to philosophy, me and the interviewer. This old guy. Professor. And I tried to show off some stuff that I'd been teaching myself about Classical . . . culture. And I was going on for ages about the Stoics [*pronounced 'stoyks'*], these Ancient Greek philosophers and their ideas, which are beautiful really. About nature and what we are to it. Ten minutes, easily, I was blathering on. Before he stopped me. And said 'Stoic. Please. It's pronounced Stoic. Get it right.' And I just . . .

Mary Are you trying to put me off now?

John No, I got in. Somewhere else. York.

Mary *nods.*

Mary OK, but how do I make it better?

John Where you wanna go?

Mary De Monfort.

John To do?

Mary Psychology. Psychology.

John OK. Do you read much? Outside what you have to?

Mary Yeah loads.

John What kinda stuff?

Mary Horror.

John OK.

Mary True Crime. Anything.

John . . .

Mary Is that not, right?

John Do you mind if I have a bit of time, think about it?

Mary You want me to go?

John   No.

Mary   I can go.

John   No seriously, I'm just. Thinking.

Mary   I hate thinking.

John   Yeah?

Mary *nods.*

John   Me too. At school, your age, I used to think – cry –
all the time.

Mary   What for?

John *shrugs.*

John   All sorts.

Mary   Gayboy.

John   Yeah, I dunno. It was. Unrequited . . . crushes.
Academic stuff. Getting upset because . . . Yeah, anything.

Mary   Do you still do it?

John   Cry?

Mary   Yeah.

John   No. Yeah. Sometimes.

Mary   Why?

John   . . .

Pause.

Mary   Are you alright?

John   What?

Mary   Are you OK?

John   . . .

Mary   I feel like. You're telling me. All these. Things.

John   Yeah.

Mary   John though.

John   What?

Mary   Are you alright?

John   Yeah.

Pause.

Mary   Where did you come back from?

John   London.

Mary   Why?

John   I was . . . I just . . .

Mary   What?

John   Everything was fine.

Mary   What you talking about?

John   I was . . .

Mary   What?

Pause.

John   Working. Living, near the river. This one evening I was out and I . . . I had this . . . I saw . . . Every part of me wanted to come home. Here. And I, I just. Started. Headed north. (*Pause.*) Woke up the next morning in Epping Forest. I was so hungry, tired. But the feeling was still there, so I carried on. Walked across motorways. Fields. Retail parks. Shop-lifted for food. The amount of burnt-out cars you see, miles from anywhere.

Mary   How long did that take?

John   Four days.

Mary   God.

John   When I turned up here I was . . . Yeah, bit of a state.

Mary   Bet.

John   Mum thought I was . . . She found me in the porch.
Blood. Mud, up me. (*Pause.*) Yeah, this isn't really helping
with your UCAS, is it?

Mary   Are you a bit . . . ?

John   . . .

Mary   Coz I'm trying to make my statement sound less
retarded.

John   I will though. I'll think about it, I'll . . . What to
write. We'll sort it out. I promise you.

Mary   Maybe I should go.

Pause.

John   Do you fancy a drink?

Mary   . . . ?

John   Dad likes his whisky. He won't mind.

Mary   It's the afternoon.

John   Yeah. It's good whisky.

Pause.

Mary *rests her bag down.*

Mary   Have you got any vodka?

Eight

The next day. Tuesday afternoon. Matalan. **Eleanor** *and* **John,**
shopping.

Eleanor   Your breath.

John   Is it bad?

Eleanor   Like a nightclub.

John   I did brush. Twice.

Eleanor   Not enough though, was it? She your new girl then?

John   Completely not.

Eleanor   Stayed late enough.

John   We weren't . . . we weren't doing any . . .

Eleanor   I don't wanna know what you were doing.

John   Mum, I wouldn't . . .

Eleanor   In my house. (*Pause*.) So what were you doing?

John   Showing her my. Photos.

Eleanor   America?

John   Yeah.

Eleanor   Love those. Grand Canyon. New York.

John *nods*.

A brief pause.

John   She's a nice girl. We just had a few drinks, and.

Eleanor   Looked at photos?

John *nods*.

John   Not a crime, is it?

Eleanor   Well, I dunno. Age of her.

John   Yeah, don't . . . she's not . . . Shall we just go and buy some shoes then?

Eleanor   Whatever you want.

John   You made me come out.

Eleanor   She was in my house, John.

John   I know.

Eleanor   Wasn't she?

John   Yes. (*Pause.*) She liked it. If that helps. The house.
I think hers is a bit.

Eleanor   Rough.

John   Maybe, yeah.

Eleanor   Where's she live?

John   St. James. Near the old Co-Op.

Eleanor   And what did she like about it?

John   Everything. All of it. The whole . . .

Eleanor   Good. Good. (*Pause.*) You changed your mind
yet? About seeing someone?

John   Mum.

Eleanor   Doctor?

John   I'm fine.

Eleanor   Clearly.

John   I just got drunk and I'd walked so far that it made
more sense ta . . . keep going.

Eleanor   Four days. Then a month in bed.

John   I'm not . . . I'm up now. I'm about. It's fine.

Eleanor   Course.

John   Yeah.

Eleanor   Well you know what I think.

John   Yes, I do.

Eleanor   About that.

John   Look, let's just buy some shoes, alright?

Eleanor   Alright. Let's.

Pause

Eleanor *exits.*

John *watches her go.*

Nine

Three days later. Friday evening. Abington Street. **Mary** *and*
Anna, *on or near a bench, facing the cash machine opposite St.
Giles Street.* **Anna** *is wearing her hooded top; the hood is up.*

Mary   Nice to meet you.

Anna *nods.*

Pause.

Mary   What is he doing?

Anna   There's a queue at the cash-point.

Mary   I know. (*Pause.*) Are you a lesbian?

Anna   Um . . .

Mary   Just that, you dress like one.

Anna   OK.

Mary   It's alright. Are you?

Anna   No.

Mary   You're straight?

Anna   Technically.

Mary   Me too. My whole life. So, have you got a boyfriend?

Anna *shakes her head.*

Mary   You out on the pull then?

Anna   No.

Mary   So what you out for? Dancing?

Anna   He just mentioned a few quiet drinks at the
Bradlaugh.

Mary   But not, me?

Anna *shakes her head.*

Mary   I'm Mary.

Anna   Yeah, I got that.

Mary   And you're. Anna.

Anna *nods.*

Mary *nods.*

Pause.

Mary   What kind of music do you like?

Anna   Trance.

Mary   Really?

Anna   No.

Mary   So. What do you like?

Anna   Anything. Apart from stuff that's shit.

Mary   Yeah, I hate stuff that's shit.

Anna   Yeah.

Mary   Like.

Mary *considers.*

Can't think of anything.

Anna   I can.

Mary   Yeah like what?

Anna   Coldplay. Toploader. Lady Gaga. Usher. Calvin
Harris. Razorlight. Sophie Ellis-Bextor. (*Pause.*) Nearly
all music, actually. Pretty much every film. Or book.
Most buildings. All people. Most climates and natural
environments. Nearly all of the other species. Quite a lot of
the planets. Then, before you get on to galaxies and all.
That. Matter, itself.

Mary   OK. Anything else?

Anna   This.

Mary   Town?

Anna *nods.*

Mary   You don't like it?

Anna *shakes her head.*

Mary   Why not?

Anna   Where do you start?

Mary   Usually on Bridge Street.

Pause.

Mary   You wanna hear a joke?

Anna *shrugs.*

Mary   How many light bulbs does it take to change a light bulb?

Anna   . . . ?

Mary   One. Funny. (*Pause.*) So how do you know him?

Anna   School.

Mary   Really? That's my school. Snap.

Anna   Right. How old are you?

Mary   Eighteen. Soon.

Anna   You're seventeen?

Mary   Only for another four months.

Anna   Magnificent.

*A passing drinker, **Ian**, walks past them. Shouts 'Tits!' whilst shoving both arms up in the air and pointing, says 'Yep' under his breath to himself, claps his hands a few times, and then, finally, is gone.*

A brief pause.

Mary   So you're not his girlfriend?

Anna *shakes her head.*

Mary   He didn't mention one, so. You're mates?

Anna   Apparently.

Mary   So. Are you worried?

Anna   What?

Mary   Worried.

Anna   About . . . ?

Mary   Him.

Anna   . . . ?

Mary   Because of all the. Stuff.

Anna   What stuff?

Mary   All of it. You know.

Anna   I don't think I do I'm asking you.

Mary   Well . . . maybe I shouldn't . . .

Anna   What stuff?

Mary   About. His. Walk.

Anna   . . . ?

Mary   From London to his parents' house. The
whole way.

Anna   What, like, for charity?

Mary   No.

Anna   I don't get . . . What do you mean?

Mary   Took him four days. He walked across country.
I think he had like a. Breakdown.

Anna   But . . .

Mary   You didn't know?

Anna   . . . (*Pause.*) How long has he known you?

Mary   About. A week.

Anna   . . .

Mary   He didn't tell you?

Anna   I . . .

Mary   No.

Anna   I . . . (*Pause.*) No.

Pause.

Mary   Did you like my joke? I made it up. On my own.

Anna   I need . . .

Mary   Are you OK?

Anna   I'm . . . I'm gonna . . .

Pause.

Anna *exits.*

A pause before **Ian** *returns.*

Ian   Darren! Darren! *OI DARREN*! *THIS WAY*! (*Pause.*)
Darren. Darren! *Darren*! Fucking . . . *DARREN*! (*To himself.*)
You deaf bastard, Darren. (*Almost doleful.*) *Darren*. Oh come
on Darren you fucker! Darren! For fuck sake!

Ian *exits.*

Pause.

Enter **John**.

John   Sorry, there were people faffing for ages.

Mary *shrugs.*

John   Where's she gone?

Mary *shakes her head.*

John *looks around.*

Mary   You could try her mobile.

John   She hasn't got one.

Mary   Really?

John *nods.*

John   Well, she'll turn up.

Mary   Will she?

John   Yeah. She knows where to find us.

Mary   OK.

Ten

Later that night. **John** *and* **Mary** *sat on the steps outside All Saints Church. They share a bottle of wine.*

Mary   The thing about people is that they don't talk to each other do they?

John   Well. You do see some people. Talking.

Mary   No no no no that's not – no – that's not what I'm saying. They don't *talk* to each other.

John   . . .

Mary   You know?

John   Um . . .

Mary   They say words and they nod and go 'Yeah yeah yeah yeah yeah' but they don't . . . they're not saying. Things. That are important.

John   It's difficult.

Mary   What is?

John   All that.

Mary   Why though?

John   I don't know.

Mary   Like my parents. They couldn't . . . They're separated.

John   Sorry.

Mary   S'alright. Probably better. He's weird, like you. Weirder. My mum thinks he's got Asperger's or something like that but he's never been diagnosed or . . . Doctors don't think he's . . . For the threshold, for that. Spectrum. So she reads all these books. All the time.

John   Psychology.

Mary   Yeah.

Mary   He said to her once, when they were together. 'You can sleep with other people, it's OK. It is.' She went *schiz* but I know he meant it. Nicely. That's how he is.

John   Weird?

Mary   *No*. Shut up. He's *nice*. He knew he wasn't making her happy so he just thought . . .

John   Someone else. Might?

Mary *nods*.

Mary   Yeah.

John   Christ.

Mary   I know. She's got so many books. Whole library.

Enter **Ian**.

Ian   Look at him he's in bits. Ain't he? He's in bits. Darren is in bits. Look at him. He's in fucking bits mate. He's in bits. Can't even. Aren't ya Darren? You're in fucking bits

mate! In. You are in bits. He's in bits. Ain't he? Oh fucking
hell, Darren, not there mate! You're gonna! No mate! *No!* I
mean it!

Ian *exits.*

John I think he's in bits.

Mary *nods.*

John You see him much? Your dad?

Mary Bit.

John Ya miss him?

Mary *shrugs.*

Mary Do you miss London?

John Bit.

Mary Maybe you should walk back.

John You reckon?

Mary See if it's still there.

John Yeah. (*Pause.*) That first morning. I couldn't
find . . . Took me ages to find even a road or . . . Almost
like I'd deliberately gone to the place where I'd be furthest
from . . .

Mary Anyone.

John Yeah.

Mary Maybe we should go back. Tonight.

John *nods.*

Mary Get pissed in a forest. Be alright.

John Why didn't you pull that guy?

Mary *shrugs.*

John Was he a bit too attractive?

Mary *nods.*

John   Yeah, I get that.

Enter **Anna**.

Mary *points out to* **John**, *with a slight head gesture, that* **Anna** *is there.*

Pause.

John   You want some?

Anna *shakes her head.*

John   Where you been?

Anna   About.

Mary *gets up.*

Mary   I think I might go to the toilet.

John   The bars are all shut.

Mary   Yeah, I meant that alley.

John   . . .

Mary *exits.*

Anna   She's young.

John   Old. Head.

Anna   Pretty.

John   I'm not . . . we're not like a . . .

Anna   I don't.

Pause.

John   What you been doing?

Anna   Dancing. On a podium. For heroin.

John   Right. Why did you shoot off?

Anna   Fucking hell.

John   Why?

Anna   Because . . .

John   Something tonight?

Anna   . . .

John   You were alright, before.

Anna   Was I?

John   Yeah. I thought . . . Yeah.

Anna *nods.*

Anna   You just don't care. Do you?

John   . . .

Anna   Think you can just . . .

Anna *shakes her head.*

Anna   Five years without . . . Anything. No contact, at all.
With me. All the ways you could have . . . To let me know
that . . . That I hadn't . . . That we still had some . . . (*Pause.*)
Then – now – suddenly you're coming round like it's . . .
Pretending you're . . . Like we're still . . . (*Pause.*) And you
tell me nothing about . . . But her. You . . . (*Pause.*) I don't
want you coming round again. I'm not a fucking . . . Am I?

Anna *nods.*

Anna   . . .

Anna *exits.*

John *drinks some wine from the bottle.*

After a while, enter **Mary.**

John   Good piss?

Mary   What she say?

John (*offering wine*)   You want some?

Mary *nods, takes the bottle.*

Ian *enters.*

Ian (*forlornly, to himself*)   Darren. Stupid bastard.
(*Spotting* **Mary**.) Hey. You.

Mary   Me?

Ian   Yeah. Yeah. You're an eight.

Mary   What?

Ian   Eight.

Mary   I don't . . .

Ian   That's all I'm saying. Aren't ya? You all are.
With your . . .

Ian *vaguely waves at* **Mary***'s body.*

Ian   It's heartbreaking. Elvis.

Ian *nods.*

Ian   Elvis Presley.

Ian *exits.*

John *and* **Mary** *watch him go.*

Mary   Bye. We should go.

John   Yeah we'll get a taxi. In a minute.

Mary *nods.*

Mary   OK.

John *reaches out, holds* **Mary***'s hand. She lets him.*

John   Great.

Mary   Yeah.

Part Two

One

The day after Part One, Scene Ten. Saturday evening. **Alan,** **Eleanor** *and* **John** *watching television.* **Alan** *is drinking bitter.*

Eleanor   What have you got it so loud for?

Alan   So I can hear it.

Eleanor *shakes her head.*

Eleanor   Hear it in Australia.

Alan   Hear you in Australia.

Eleanor   Right. Right.

Eleanor *shakes her head.*

Pause.

You're in then?

John   What?

Eleanor   Tonight?

John   Yeah.

Eleanor   Saturday night. Not seeing Anna?

John *shakes his head.*

Eleanor   Or that new one?

John *shakes his head.*

Eleanor   Lolita.

John   No, she's busy.

Eleanor   Right.

Alan (*referring to TV Harry Hill*)   Fight!

Alan *laughs.*

John *smiles a little.*

Eleanor   Quite a shock that. Coming down this morning, seeing her in the kitchen. Eating our Alpen. In your dressing gown.

John   Mum, I told you. I slept on the floor. She had the bed.

Eleanor   Did she?

John   Yes.

Eleanor   Well. Didn't know what to think, let alone say to her.

John   She said you were very polite.

Eleanor   Of course I was. What am I gonna do, set fire to her in the kitchen? Hack her fingers off?

John   No, but she, appreciated it. And she said you were nice as well Dad.

Alan   Yeah.

Eleanor   Thought you'd gone out with Anna.

John   I did. We bumped into Mary, while we were out.

Eleanor   Convenient.

Alan   El.

Eleanor   What?

Alan   Ellie.

Eleanor   I'm having a conversation with my son, what are you doing?

Alan   Minding my own.

Eleanor   Oh. Are you? Doesn't sound like it, though I wouldn't know *as I can't hear you over the noise of the television.*

Eleanor *shakes her head. Sighs.*

They all watch television.

Eleanor   She is very young, that's all I'm saying.

Alan   Well you've said it now, haven't ya?

Eleanor   . . .

Eleanor *shakes her head.*

They all watch television.

John   Dad. Can I get a drink?

Alan *nods.*

Alan   Beer?

John *nods.*

Alan   By the back door.

John   Ta.

John *gets up and exits.*

Pause.

Eleanor   How's your knee?

Alan   Still there.

Eleanor   And the swelling?

Alan *nods.*

Alan   Swell.

Eleanor *smiles a little.*

Eleanor   You berk.

Alan   You're the one that married it.

Eleanor   Yeah.

They share a slight smile.

A pause before **John** *enters with his beer.*

Alan   It's Belgian. Creamy.

John   Is it?

Alan *nods.*

John *sits.*

Alan   Nice. Cheap enough.

John *drinks.*

Eleanor   Has she ever worn make-up?

John   Who?

Eleanor   Anna.

John   Don't think so.

Eleanor *nods.*

Eleanor   Suppose she doesn't need to, her skin.

Alan   Radiant.

Eleanor   Yeah. Still down Lodge farm, is she?

John   Yes.

Eleanor   Data something?

John   Entry, yeah.

Eleanor   Data entry.

John *nods.*

Eleanor *nods.*

Pause.

Eleanor   Your hair needs cutting. Dad'll take ya.

Alan   What?

John   I'm alright.

Eleanor   John, you look like a gypsy.

John   It's fine.

Eleanor   Well.

Alan   How's all the school stuff?

John   They said I could help out when I want but I might do a few shifts this week.

Eleanor   Work?

John   Yeah. Called them today, talked to Vinnie. He's gonna pull a few strings.

Eleanor   You're going back?

John   Yeah.

Alan   Bit of exercise. Good for ya.

John   Hopefully.

Eleanor   Well don't over do it.

John   It's not exactly labouring.

Eleanor   I know.

John   It's retail.

Eleanor   I know. But if it's a money thing, we can help ya.

Alan   Yeah.

John   No. It isn't.

Pause.

Eleanor   Well you'll have to get a haircut if you're dealing with the public.

John   Mum.

Eleanor   Paying customers. They'll expect a bit more of ya. Won't they?

Pause.

John   How's Elizabeth?

Alan   Oi.

Eleanor   What?

John   How is she? (*Pause.*) How's it look now? I've not been there. Years.

Eleanor   . . .

John   Do you take her flowers?

Eleanor   . . .

John   What do you do there? Thought you wanted to talk to me.

Eleanor   No, I don't.

John   No.

Alan   J.

John   It was a question.

Alan   I don't care.

John   That's all.

Alan   John.

They watch television in silence.

John   I like this beer. Dad, can I take a few, drink 'em up in my room?

Alan   Yeah.

John   Thank you.

John *exits.*

They watch television. **Alan** *looks to* **Eleanor** *but she doesn't return the look.*

Eleanor   Don't.

Two

Four days later. Wednesday afternoon. Homebase, on the Weedon Road. An isolated aisle. **John** *sat on a foot-stool, fiddling with a Stanley knife.* **Anna**, *standing away from him.*

Anna   I went round yours. Your dad made me Vimto.

John   OK.

Anna   And gave me some Hula Hoops. In a bowl. Told me you were here.

John   Yeah.

Anna   Surprise.

John *nods.*

Anna *nods.*

Anna   What are you doing?

John   The blade's blunt.

Anna   No. Here.

John   Working.

Anna   Yeah I know that why?

No response.

Anna   And why aren't you green anymore?

John   They changed it.

Anna   Idiots. I loved the green. Could see you for miles.

John   Yeah.

Anna   That amazing orange collar.

John   Thought you were angry. With me.

Anna   I am. Just miss the uniform.

John   I'm sort of done, talking about things, I think.

Anna   OK, but we didn't.

John   Best thing about here.

Anna   We haven't.

John   You only ever get asked about rawlplugs. Or dado rails.

Anna   I could ask you about dado rails.

John   Alright.

Anna   . . . (*Pause.*) Your dad was very nice. Though he did tell me that all Somalis look the same. Even to each other, apparently. Something to do with the shape of their heads. Yeah I don't think he's right about that.

John *shrugs.*

Anna   I can't imagine a whole race of people going, 'Er, do I know you? I'm great with names, terrible with faces. As we all are.' You wouldn't get anything done.

John   No.

Anna   Would you?

John *shakes his head.*

Anna   I wouldn't, anyway. (*Pause.*) So are you enjoying. Homebase?

John   It's my second shift. Like I've never been away.

Anna   OK.

John   But at least it's not home. Or anywhere else.

Anna *nods.*

Pause.

Anna   Thought I would say hello.

John   You have.

Anna   Make an effort.

John   Yeah.

Anna   Be an adult, about it. You make our friendship quite difficult, sometimes.

John   Do I?

Anna   Has been known.

John   And you don't?

Anna   What? The wedding?

John *nods.*

Anna   Five years ago, and we were both so. Drunk.

John   I know.

Anna   I just kissed you, that's all. And you ran away.

John   Yeah.

Anna   And. Do you know how I found out? That you'd gone?

John *shrugs.*

Anna   My mum. She met yours in Debenhams, 'bout a month later. She told her that you'd moved out, down to. In Pimlico, some flat-share. Assumed I knew. That I'd be visiting you, all the time.

John   You shouldn't have . . . The things you were saying. And I wanted to move, anyway.

Anna   Right.

John   Yeah, I really didn't wanna hang round here and . . .

Anna   What?

John   Fall apart.

Anna   Worked well that. Didn't it?

John   Fuck off.

Anna   OK.

John   Please.

Anna   You're such a little boy.

John   Least I'm not . . .

Anna   What?

John   A fucking waste.

Anna   Right.

John   Yeah. And we're in the middle of a stock-take, so.

Anna   Well, good luck with that.

John   Thank you.

Anna   Yeah.

John   Yeah.

Anna   You fucking. Prick.

Three

Two days later. Thursday evening. The Fat Cat bar on Bridge Street. **John** *and* **Mary**, *drinking. Loud, pounding music plays.*

John   Jesus.

Mary   What?

John   Not been here ages.

Mary   One of the best places to start.

John   Is it?

Mary *nods.*

John   Is that because it makes everywhere else seem better?

Mary   No.

They drink.

John   At the bar, there were about thirty guys, all chanting the A-Team theme tune.

Mary   OK.

John   I've never seen people so pleased with themselves.

Mary   OK.

John   These idiots.

Mary   Right.

John   Aren't they?

Mary *shrugs.*

John *shakes his head.*

John   All of them.

Pause. They drink.

Mary   Saw my dad this weekend. In Leicester. Why I couldn't meet up.

John   OK. You finished your UCAS yet?

Mary *shakes her head.*

Mary   My dad thinks we're all gonna. Starve. Like all the people in the world.

John   Yeah, we might.

Mary   You think that?

John   Eventually.

Mary   He thinks soon, though. That, there isn't any. Hope.

John   Fair enough.

Mary   It's not . . . You don't know what it's like. Hearing your dad say things like that.

John   No.

A brief pause.

John   What is it, like?

Mary   Horrible. And my mum. She's talking about moving away.

John   OK.

Mary   Yeah, she says she needs some space. To think about her life.

John   Where's she wanna go?

Mary   Guildford. She's got a boyfriend there. From Facebook.

John   Well you be alright. Off to uni, so.

Mary   No. I can't.

John   What?

Mary   A-Levels.

John   What about 'em?

Mary   I can't do it. Too hard. Might have to drop out.

John   Well I can help you, if you're struggling.

Mary   Not enough. I just never know what to write, about anything. And when I do, it's. Retarded.

A brief pause.

John   Your friends could help you out.

Mary   Haven't really got any. Usually just have boyfriends. Hang round with their friends.

John   OK. Right.

Mary   So . . .

John   I'm working now.

Mary   OK.

John   Homebase.

Mary . . .

John Weedon Road.

Mary *nods.*

John It's alright.

Mary *nods.*

They drink.

John They're gonna train me how to use the.

Mary OK.

John Forklift.

Mary *nods.*

John Quite an expensive course.

Enter **Ian**.

Ian Hello.

John What?

Ian Hello.

John . . . ?

Ian Spoils of war.

Ian *smiles broadly.*

John What?

Ian That's all it is mate.

John Right.

Ian Ain't it?

John Um . . .

Ian All of it.

Ian *nods, puts his drink down.*

John   We're actually . . .

Ian   What?

John   Talking.

Ian   Yeah don't mind me.

Mary   We were.

Ian   Alright love.

A pause, during which they all drink.

Busy tonight. Well busy.

John *nods*.

Ian   Too many men here though. Bit. Cock-heavy. Ain't it?

Ian *nods to himself.*

Though I prefer that, sometimes. (*To* **Mary**.) I tell you what. You could do better.

Mary   . . . ?

Ian   A lot better. I'm a gentleman. Gentle.

John   Sorry.

Ian   What for?

John   We were talking.

Ian   Yeah, you were.

John   No. We're friends.

Ian   You won't mind then will ya?

John   Well . . . I do, actually.

Ian   We all do mate. How about you fucking grow some?

Mary (*to* **John**)   It's alright.

Ian   Course it is. So what's your name lovely?

Mary   Kylie.

Ian   Kylie. And what do you do darling?

Mary   I'm fourteen.

Ian   Right.

Mary   So I'm at school. GCSEs.

Ian   Yeah and who's this, your dad?

Mary   No, he's my . . . He works in London.

Ian   Do ya?

John   Well, I did yeah.

Ian   What, on a gay farm?

John   No. In an office.

Ian   A gay office?

John   No.

Ian   So what you do there, wank-off all day in your gay suit?

John   Human Resources.

Ian   . . . ?

John   Admin. But I left.

Ian   Bet you did.

John   Yeah.

Ian   So you're a right couple o'cunts then? Schoolgirl and a fat-cat paedo. Party town.

John   Look.

Mary   We were talking.

John   Do you mind?

Ian   Na na you should mind, mate. You should. Yeah. I got my fucking eyes on you, alright?

John   Right.

Ian   And I tell you what.

John   What?

Ian   Seven phone-calls.

John   . . . ?

Ian   Seven.

John   To do what?

Ian   What?

John   Seven phone-calls to do what?

Ian   Take. You. Out.

John   Seven?

Ian   Yeah.

John   Right.

Ian   Exactly. And I got a phone. On me.

John   Yeah.

Ian *nods*.

Ian   Speed-dial.

John   OK.

Ian   Yeah.

John   Great.

Ian   Think about that.

Ian *turns to* **Mary**.

Pause. They drink.

Ian   You have excellent legs.

Mary   I know.

John   OK.

Ian   What?

John   Call them.

Ian   What ya saying?

John   Fuck it. Call them.

Ian   Yeah?

John   Yeah.

Ian   You're gone mate.

John *laughs a bit.*

John   Right. This whole place. Please. Call.

Ian   Yeah. You wait.

John   I will.

Ian *backs away.*

Ian   I'm everywhere. All the time. (*To* **Mary**.) And you'll be back. Legs. All day.

Ian *nods.*

Yeah.

Ian *exits.*

John   Brilliant. (*Pause.*) Guys like that.

Mary   Are we friends?

John   What?

Mary   Are we?

John   Course.

Mary *nods.*

Mary   I didn't know you worked in a office.

John   Well I did.

Mary   I was gonna tell him you were a scientist. Famous one.

John   Right.

Mary   Invented something.

John   Discovered.

Mary   Yeah.

A brief pause.

John   You're not actually fourteen?

Mary   *No.*

John   Course. No.

Mary   You can be so stupid.

John   Yeah.

They drink.

John   One day, all these people will be dead.

Mary   What?

John   Won't they?

Mary *nods.*

John   And us.

Mary *nods.*

Mary   OK.

John   You must get a lot of guys like that. Coming up to you.

Mary *shrugs.*

John   You like it?

Mary   Sometimes.

John   Guys like that?

Mary   Not everyone's like that.

John   Show me someone here, who isn't.

Mary   Us.

John   And you shouldn't encourage 'em.

Mary   I didn't.

John   Girls like you. They breed off it.

Mary   Girls like what?

John   You.

Mary   Stop it.

John   No. I'm explaining. How this all works. How it all fucking works. I've seen the way you talk to them.

Mary   OK.

John   Haven't I?

Mary   Yeah. But I don't think you were listening.

Pause.

John   I fancy some shots.

Mary *shakes her head.*

Mary   OK.

John   Yeah. I wanna get smashed.

John *exits.*

Mary *looks around the bar. Drinks.*

Four

The music from the nightclub distorts into that from the beginning of Part One.

We see **John** *drinking, shot after shot.*

Then **John**, *alone in town. Suddenly he sees* **Thomas**, *under water, floating in front of him.* **John** *moves towards him. He vanishes.*

John *is alone. He walks across the stage, unable to find his way.*

Five

Early the next morning. The kitchen. It is raining outside. **Alan** *enters, carrying a dressing gown and towel. Turns the light on. Puts the gown/towel to one side. Takes out some newspaper (stored for recycling), lays it out on the floor. Then picks up a key and opens the back door. Lets* **John** *in.*

John *is a drunken mess, covered in anti-climb paint, blood and rain.*

Alan   State of ya. Come on. Get it off.

John   What?

Alan   Your top. New, innit? Ain't letting your mum see that.

John   OK.

Alan   We'll tell her you lost it.

John *nods, takes his top off, drops it on the newspaper.* **Alan** *dries him with the towel.*

Alan   Come on.

John   I can . . . do it.

Alan   No, you bloody can't.

Alan *continues to dry him.*

Alan   So what happened?

John *shakes his head.*

Alan   Fall over?

John *shrugs.*

John . . .

Alan Fight?

John *shrugs.*

Alan Well summat did.

John Nothing.

Alan State of ya. If she saw you.

John I know.

Alan Break her up.

John I know.

Alan So why'd you keep fucking doing it?

No response.

Here.

Alan *hands him the dressing gown.*

Alan Take it. Look at ya.

John *shakes his head.*

Alan I don't see ya.

John Dad.

Alan Eh?

John *shakes his head.*

Alan Who is it? In there?

John . . .

Alan Look at ya. (*Pause.*) What's all this black stuff?

John Anti . . . climb . . . paint.

Alan Well that worked then, didn't it?

John . . .

Alan Your blood? Just yours?

John *nods.*

Alan Right. You ain't a child.

John Yeah.

Alan And I ain't . . . Can't keep . . .

John Dad.

Alan Can we? There's gotta be a point.

John Please.

Alan Where you grip it.

John I'm . . .

Alan Ain't there?

Alan *nods.*

John *nods.*

John I just wanna sleep.

Alan OK then.

Alan *nods.*

Alan But keep it down. We're not waking her. Are we? Not tonight.

John *shakes his head.*

Alan Good job I was up.

John *nods.*

John Sorry.

Alan Yeah. (*Pause.*) You know what my Auntie used to say?

John *shakes his head.*

Alan 'Don't waste your time worrying. Worry about wasting your time.'

John   OK.

Alan   Yeah. Though she was a mad old bitch. Irish. Proper Irish. Slept with a lot of American soldiers in the war. A lot.

John *nods.*

Alan   Tough as you like. The mouth on her. She was horrible to me.

John   Why?

Alan   Jealous.

John   What of?

Alan   Coz I was the oldest. Favourite. I came along, spoiled things.

John   . . . ?

Alan   Because she missed my mum. I took her away. Stole her. Her time, with her. So she was all on her own. Poor old girl. Rose. (*Pause.*) Come on bed.

Six

The next day. Early evening. Friday. The living room. **Eleanor** *and* **John**, *sat playing Scrabble.* **John** *wears his dressing gown.*

Silence.

Eleanor   Nice lie-in?

John *nods.*

Eleanor   Yeah.

Eleanor *puts down her letters.*

John   What's that mean?

Eleanor   A gap in knowledge.

John   Never heard of it.

Eleanor   Look it up, don't believe me.

She counts her score, jots it down and picks new letters. Then she swivels the board round to **John***.*

John   Got five Is.

Eleanor   Shush, shouldn't tell me.

John *shakes his head.*

John   Rubbish. Utter . . .

A long pause. **John** *is toying with his letters.*

John   Nothing.

Eleanor   Stop it. Have a go.

John   Can't.

Eleanor   Try.

John   Really.

Eleanor   Something short. Simple.

John   Can I skip a go?

Eleanor   Please.

John   Fuck sake. (*Sighs.*) Alright.

John *lays out his letters.*

Counting his score.

Eleanor   Eight. Told ya.

John   Mum you're fixty-six points ahead o' me.

Eleanor   Forty-eight now.

John *sighs.*

John *writes down his score, takes out new letters, swivels the board back.*

John   I'm sure I used to beat you occasionally.

Eleanor   Can't recall.

John   And it's definitely not fair you've memorised all the two-letter fucking words.

Eleanor   Knowledge isn't cheating, John.

John   . . .

Eleanor   Is it?

John *shakes his head.*

Eleanor   You look a bit tired.

John   Yeah.

Eleanor   Big night?

John *nods.*

Eleanor   Need to be careful.

John   I know.

Eleanor   Don't want a repeat. I'm struggling.

John   I didn't wake you up? Last night?

Eleanor   No, I was sound off. Too many Gs. You had a falling out? With Anna? Have ya?

John   I . . .

Eleanor   What?

John   I'm . . .

Pause.

Eleanor   John. John.

John   Yeah.

Eleanor   Please.

John   I don't . . . I'm not . . .

Eleanor   John.

John   Am I?

Eleanor   No. Breathe.

John   I am.

Eleanor   Deeper. Please.

A long pause.

John   Things are a bit. With Anna. And it's easier to. With everything. Cut things off.

Eleanor   It's not.

John   Make things more . . . Simple.

Eleanor   Cut you from me, day you were born. And Elizabeth.

John   . . .

Eleanor   Don't make it easier.

John   Mum.

Eleanor   Or simple. Not one bit.

Pause.

Eleanor *lays out her letters.*

Counts them.

Seventeen. And I cheated.

She jots this down, turns the board around.

John   Still got four Is.

Eleanor   Yeah.

John   This game.

Eleanor   You need to see someone, you know that. Talk to
someone. And I know it's not me. I know you couldn't, with
me. I do know that.

John   . . .

Eleanor   But it's still in there. Something. And if you don't.
Properly. It'll happen again. Keep happening. She's your
best friend. In the whole world. Since you were little. If not
a doctor, you won't. Her?

John   Maybe.

Eleanor   And I know it's my fault.

John   No.

Eleanor   Way, we never talked. About your sister. I just
never could.

John   Mum.

Eleanor   Don't think I ever will. Elizabeth was . . . Finding
her, like that. In her cot.

John   Yeah.

Eleanor   Too . . . The end of your world, somehow.

John *nods.*

Silence.

John   I'll talk to her. Anna.

John *turns his letters to face* **Eleanor**.

John   As long as you help me with that.

Eleanor   Oh dear.

John   Yeah.

Eleanor   What a mess.

John *nods.*

Eleanor   You should a' skipped a go.

Seven

*Later. Friday evening. The sky is blue/black. An alleyway, leading
to the centre of Duston. Next to the old Timken site (now a new
housing estate).* **Anna** *and* **John**.

Anna   You see it?

John   Yeah.

Anna   That tower. They built it for all the young
professionals. Centre of town. Swimming pool. Balconies.
Gym. They started at like two hundred thousand pounds
for these one or two beds. Unfortunately, they didn't realise
that there aren't any young professionals in Northampton.
So about three people brought them and then the council
rented out the rest to asylum seekers. You can get one now
for about seventy grand.

John   Fuck.

Anna   Yeah. And I like it, like this. When there's only two
or three lights on. Imagine those young couples who
thought, 'Wow. This'll be like living in. New York. London.
Shanghai.' And now they're fucking in. Mogadishu.

John *nods*.

Pause.

John   Didn't think you'd come out.

Anna *shrugs*.

Anna   My sister's round. She was showing us her film she's
edited of the latest Christening. James. Which I was actually
at. Anything, to get out.

John   Even me.

Anna   Yeah.

Silence.

John   I'm not sure that I'm . . . alright.

Anna   OK.

John   You know?

John   They way I get.

Anna *nods*

Anna   Amount of parties I've had to drag you out of. Coz you've lost it at someone, or.

John *nods.*

John   I got down before, but now. These last few years. I mean, I look forward. The future. I don't see . . . Anything.

Anna   Right.

John   Of anything. (*Pause.*) I spent five years in London, hoping I could just. Keep my head down. And I did. Got through work by pretending it was temporary. Through evenings by. Drinking. Just that. Weekends, I'd walk round Leicester Square, Covent Garden. Anywhere central. In these circles. On my own. (*Pause.*) All that time trying to sit things out. Then you look forward. And you think, if this is five, how can I last another fifty? (*Pause.*) The last day I was there. I was on Vauxhall Bridge. It was the afternoon. I should have been at work. And I saw this guy. Get off a bus. Walk along, towards me. Calm as you like. Climbed up, onto the side of the bridge. Then stepped off. Into the Thames. It was so . . . Easy. The way he dropped. Fell. And all I could think was. 'Why not?' So I started walking, to get away from that answer.

Anna   Did he die?

John   I think so. Though I'm not entirely sure that I saw it.

Anna   Oh. Fuck.

John   Yeah. I saw other things. On the walk. Can't work out what were dreams and what was . . .

Anna   Like what?

John   Stars collapsing. With me inside them. There were
points where I felt like I was underwater. On the river-bed.
Looking – directly – at the guy who jumped. Once I woke
up in a barn. At night. Pitch-black. I thought it was a coffin.
Genuinely. That I had been buried, underground. . . . I was
ripping at this wood, trying to get out. Thought I was
gonna die. I really did. Woke up my hands, were . . . My
face. (*Pause.*) I think I might be in trouble.

Anna   Yeah.

John   Yeah.

Silence.

Anna   You've always been so . . .

John   What?

Anna   Delicate. Remember at school, you were always
storming off, when people said things. Little things but off
you'd go, sit in the toilets, cry, for hours.

John   Yeah.

Anna   Why I liked you.

John   What?

Anna   You couldn't pretend, like everyone else. You
couldn't go along with all the. Why I first sat next to you in
French.

John   I thought you wanted to copy my coursework.

Anna   That as well. Oui.

Pause.

John   I did miss the skies here. The fucker about London
you can never see it, properly.

Anna   Here, all you can see.

John   Yeah.

Pause.

Anna   You gonna speak to anyone? Like, a doctor?

John   I don't know. Maybe.

Anna   Well, I'll go with you, if you.

John   OK.

Anna   Yeah. Whatever you want. Always.

John   Thank you. Yeah. (*Pause.*) It's four, apparently. The perfect size, for a crew. To get to another planet. Through space. Two men, two women. And they all have to be from the same culture.

Anna   Right.

John   Can you imagine us in space?

Anna   No. Though if we were, I'd feel a bit fucking sorry for the other two.

John   Yeah.

Anna   Unless they were French. (*Pause.*) You'll be alright. I promise.

John   OK.

Anna   In fifty years time, we'll still be the most awkward bastards on the whole planet.

John   I hope so.

Anna   Watching *Seinfeld* together the whole way through for the fortieth time.

John   Yeah.

Anna   Spending the last of our, space pension on, space Pringles.

John   Right.

Anna   And space salsa dip.

John   Can I have space sour cream?

Anna   Of course. Milked from space cats.

Pause.

John   Anna. About the kiss. I don't want you to think that . . .

Anna   It's OK. Maybe another night.

John   OK.

Anna   Yeah. We've got enough of them. (Pause.) Haven't we?

John   Yeah.

Anna   Well then.

Eight

The next day. Saturday afternoon. The Grosvenor Centre. Upstairs. **Mary** *sat on a bench on the through-fare. She drinks from a small McDonald's Diet Coke.*

Enter **Alan** *and* **Eleanor**. **Alan** *notices her first.*

Alan   Hello.

Mary   What?

Alan   I made you a Ribena. You was eating our Alpen.

Mary   Yeah.

Alan   Y'alright?

Mary   . . .

Mary *nods.*

Alan   Been shopping?

Mary   No. Just. McDonald's. Happy Meal.

Alan   Cheap.

Mary *nods.*

Alan   We're just having a wander. Been all over. Out on your own?

Mary *looks around a bit. Nods.*

Eleanor   Quiet today. For a Saturday.

Mary *nods.*

Alan   Yeah, quiet.

Mary   Less people.

Alan   Exactly. (*Pause.*) Need some company?

Alan *sits next to* **Mary** *on the bench.*

Mary   What?

Eleanor   Alan.

Alan   Well we could do with a rest. Miles, we've been.

Mary   Erm. OK.

Eleanor   If that's . . . alright?

Mary *nods.*

Eleanor *sits down on the other side of* **Mary.**

Alan   Watch the world go by.

Eleanor   Take the weight off.

Mary *nods.*

Pause.

Eleanor   So you weren't shopping then?

Mary *shakes her head.*

Eleanor   Just in town?

Mary *nods.*

Eleanor   Good to be out. And about.

Mary *nods.*

Mary   I like your house.

Eleanor   I know. He said.

Alan   Moved down in seventy-five. From London. Streatham.

Mary   Wow.

Eleanor   Thirty-five years, that house.

Mary   Ages. Looks like. New.

Eleanor   Yeah. Apart from the carpets.

Eleanor *flicks a look at* **Alan**. *He doesn't notice.*

Eleanor   I said, apart from the carpets.

Alan   Don't start girl.

Eleanor   Apart from them, yeah.

Mary   I like it.

Eleanor   Thank you. Nice of you. Rough day?

Mary   What?

Eleanor   Rough. Has it?

Mary   Erm . . .

Eleanor   Difficult.

Mary *shrugs.*

Eleanor   Don't worry though, you'll be alright. Won't she?

Alan   Yeah.

Eleanor   Yeah.

Mary   OK.

Eleanor   You'll see.

Silence, but for the bustle.

Mary   I'm thinking about moving away.

Eleanor   For university? He said you were applying.

Mary   No. Forever.

Eleanor   Where to?

Mary   Don't know. Somewhere.

Eleanor   Alright.

Mary   Maybe Scotland. Wales. Somewhere. The country.

Alan   Can't beat nature.

Mary   No yeah.

Alan   Fresh air. Hills. Sheep. Rivers. Yeah.

Mary *nods.*

Eleanor   You want us to go? We bothering you?

Mary   No. Stay.

Eleanor   Yeah?

Mary   Yeah. Or maybe I should get somewhere. In town. On my own.

Silence, but for the bustle.

Mary   What sort of music do you like?

Eleanor   Film soundtracks.

Alan   *Fist Full of Dollars.* Very Good.

Alan *whistles it.*

Mary   I like anything, as long as it has words. Lyrics.

Eleanor   Course.

Mary   Motown. I like that. My mum likes that.

Eleanor   Diana Ross. Supremes.

Mary   Yeah. (*Pause.*) I only ever been here.

Eleanor   Born and bred?

Mary   My whole life. And I don't know anyone. Not really.

Eleanor   Course you do.

Mary   No. No-one. Who'll stay, with me.

Eleanor   Shame.

Mary   I know. Yeah.

Silence, but for the bustle. They watch the world go by.

Eleanor   Well. You still hungry?

Mary *smiles.*

Nine

Later. Saturday afternoon. **John**'s *bedroom.* **Mary** *and* **John**. *They stand.*

Mary   Your parents gave me a lift back. I wouldn't have come, otherwise.

John   It's OK.

Mary   Is it?

John *nods.*

Mary   You left.

John   Yeah.

Mary   Walked off. That guy came back. Gave me all this shit. Loads. (*Pause.*) Had to get a taxi back. On my self.

John   I'm sorry.

Mary   You said some horrible things.

John   Yeah. I get like that.

Mary   Why?

John   Because of how I am.

Mary   And what's that?

John   I don't know yet.

Mary *nods.*

Pause.

Mary   Your mum's making me dinner.

John   Really?

Mary *nods.*

John   OK.

Pause

John   You still gonna drop out?

Mary   Don't know. Maybe.

John   Either way. I drafted you a statement. UCAS. It's pretty good

Mary   OK.

Pause.

Mary   You grew up in this room, didn't you?

John   Yeah.

Mary   All your life?

John *nods.*

John   Though for the first few weeks. I shared it.

Mary   With?

John   My sister. Elizabeth.

Mary   You have a sister?

John   No. She died. Something to do with her heart. Four weeks old. After that, Mum and Dad couldn't face . . . trying again. Why it's just me.

Mary *nods.*

Pause.

Mary   Have you got any music?

John   Bit.

Mary   With lyrics. Please.

John *nods. Goes to his stereo. Puts on 'Our Way To Fall' by Yo La Tengo.*

They listen.

Mary   It's good. Where are the words?

John   Just a minute. Any second.

The lyrics start. **Mary** *moves a little to the music.*

John   It is rather good. They're American.

Mary   We could dance. If you weren't such a shitbag.

John   Yeah.

Mary   Couldn't we?

John *nods.*

They listen to the music.

John *moves towards her. Surprises her by blowing a raspberry on her forehead.*

Mary   Get off.

John   Still wanna dance?

Mary   No. You fucking bumboy.

John   Yeah. (*Pause.*) I'm sorry.

Mary   OK.

John   I really am.

John *moves forward, maybe to dance with* **Mary**.

Instead, **Mary** *stands on his feet and they dance together.* **John** *leads.*

Ten

Later. Early Saturday evening. **Alan,** **Eleanor** *and* **Mary** *sat watching the television.* **John,** *standing, away from them.*

Alan   Attenborough. He knows what he's doing. Very clever.

Eleanor   Their little faces.

Mary   What's it doing?

Alan   Dunno. Smiling? Something. They eat each other. Monkeys.

Eleanor   They don't.

Alan   They do.

Eleanor   Alan.

Alan   I seen it. (*Pause.*) And they throw their shit about.

Silence.

John   Erm. I was gonna go round Anna's.

Eleanor   Right.

Mary   OK.

John (*To* **Mary**.)   You wanna come?

Mary   Um . . .

Eleanor   It's alright.

Mary   No. I wanna stay.

John   Yeah?

Mary   Yeah.

John   OK.

Alan   You taking a coat?

John   I will.

Alan   Good.

Eleanor   You got your key?

John   Yeah, I might be a bit late.

Eleanor   Alright. We'll leave the latch off.

John   Great.

John *exits.*

They watch television.

Honest

Honest was produced by Royal & Derngate at the Mailcoach pub in Northampton and first performed on 26 February 2010. The cast was as follows:

Dave   Thomas Morrison

Director   Mike Bartlett

Characters

Dave

Notes

This play does not necessarily need to be performed in a traditional theatre space.

The details of the play can and probably should be changed, here and there, to represent the physicality, age, background and location (in time and space) of the actor who performs it.

*'You know I hate, detest, and can't bear a lie, not because
I am straighter than the rest of us, but simply because it
appals me. There is a taint of death, a flavour of mortality
in lies – which is exactly what I hate and detest in the
world – what I want to forget.'*

Marlow in Joseph Conrad's
Heart of Darkness (1902)

'The art of art is to flirt, or hurt; never instruct.'

Werner Herzog in *Conversations
with Death and her Mother* (1989)

I think I'm probably a bit of cunt, to be honest.

As I get older, it gets harder to lie. To tell lies to make people feel better about themselves.

I can't do it.

I won't.

And I know that lying is generally associated with cunts – 'You lying cunt,' etcetera – but I think that's wrong, actually. Because cunts – usually – will tell you what they think. The truth.

That's why – on the whole – you try to avoid them.

And lately, the best I can do is:

Hold back.

Like.

My nephew – my nephew, Ben – showed me this drawing he'd done. Of a tiger, a tiger attacking a bus. And it was terrible. Awful. Even for his age, and a few years ago I would've said, you know, 'Well done, Ben, that's much better than what I could do, when I was ten.'

But . . .

It wasn't.

I mean, I was pretty good – I won some prizes – and his, was . . .

. . .

Yet, I couldn't lie to him.

I couldn't bring myself to . . .

. . .

So I just. Walked away.

Left him there, in the garden. Waving his drawing about.

Ben.

Pause.

Work has also been . . .

I work for the Government, down in London, at the Department of Inclusion and Social Affairs. In this big modern glass . . . wanky fucking . . . toss . . . building, just behind Victoria. And I work in this section called the Strategic and Tactical Development Team.

Yeah. STD.

T.

And if you've ever worked in the Civil Service – anywhere like that, really – you'll know that the word that is most solidly abused – along with 'community' and 'ethnic' – is, er: 'strategic'.

Honestly, if you replace the word 'strategic' in most Government reports with the word 'anus', just in your head, they – nearly always – make much more sense. Because then at least they relate to something, out here, in the real world. That. Exists.

Anuses.

And 'tactical' gets abused less but the people who really . . . get their fingers in, with 'strategic', tend to throw in 'tactical' a lot, even though they mean completely opposite things and effectively, cancel each other out.

'Development' doesn't mean anything at all, at least not in a Government context. 'Team' just means more than one person. Yeah so the STD.T could be called. Er . . . Some Humans Trying To Work Out What's Going On. And That.

(*Pronouncing it as one word.*) SHTTWOWGOAT.

Which I quite like.

But someone, somewhere – some faceless . . . – came up with Strategic and Tactical Development Team.

I joined nine months ago and probably the single most frustrating thing is that. I don't understand. On nearly any level. What they're meant to be doing.

I mean, I do know it's linked to inclusion policy.

I'm a bit of an expert on social inclusion. I would never say that at a party or anything – it's not very sexy really – but yeah. I am. So, I. I know how disinclined we all are, to . . . How much we like to stick together, with our own – whether that's race or class, or both – despite everything we know about . . . Like, how money used to support different groups, actually helps to, to segregate them. How. How there are third and fourth generation children born in this country with no real understanding of, of our language. Culture.

Yeah, it's difficult to pull with that kind of stuff, really.

Pause.

The boss, my boss in the STD.T is also called Ben and he's this . . .

Colossal . . .

. . .

He's got a PhD in Chemistry from Bristol, I think. Or, Durham. Somewhere posh and very white that isn't Cambridge or Oxford but very much wants to be.

And Ben loves data. He's great with data, apparently. Everyone always says that.

Unfortunately – from my own experience – he's awful with. Words. Ideas.

Talking, writing, listening. Thinking. He – leading, managing – he can't, or won't, do any of them.

He – Ben, right? – sat me down for two hours, when I first joined, and I did, I asked him quite a lot of questions. When I could.

And what I got in response was continually along the lines of:

'Well yeah – yeah – what we what we aim for here is to draw in, draw in all the hard data, over-lay that that with – cross-reference it, merge it – with all the the soft information out there – pull it all together, see what we've got – and then provide provide both a strategic and tactical overview understanding overview for for the stakeholders – customers – across Whitehall. Yeah. Yeah. That's. That's what we do here.'

He nods.

Pause.

Jesus Christ.

When he said that. When he kept saying that, in increasingly meaningless ways.

I mean, he looked so pleased with himself. Sat there, opposite me.

Like, a retarded fourteen-year-old Emperor. With a hard on.

Sat in your fridge.

Wanking – really fucking wanking – into your newly bought tub of Flora.

But for the two hours, I just – at least outwardly – nodded. Asked questions when I could.

(*Nodding.*) 'Yeah.'

'That makes . . . that seems to make . . . '

'I . . . yeah.'

'Yeah.'

'Of course.'

'*Yes*, that's . . . '

'Yeah.'

'Right.'

He nods.

'OK.'

'Is it?'

He nods.

Pause.

He exhales.

Part of my job. Pretty much all of my job. In the STD.T, is to sign-off reports for all the analysts in Ben's team. And the analysts are . . .

. . .

When I was a kid, I was in the Boys' Brigade, which, for those of you who don't know, is like a militant, Christian Scouts. Less fun, probably around the same level of tacit, latent paedophilia. And at the time, I asked my brother, who was older than me – still is – and very hard, popular, gelled his hair a lot, sometimes used my Mum's hairspray but pretended – denied very strongly – that he ever did. I asked him, why everyone at Boys' Brigade was either really fat, or, really thin.

And he said:

'Because in everyone in Boys' Brigade is a fucking geek.'

He nods and smiles a little.

And he was right.

The STD.T analysts are the same.

And I've seen this before in the Department and other bits of Government I've visited or worked with. You get these pockets of unadulterated incompetence, areas where odd behaviour and characters have kind of. Evolved. Uniquely, over time. In many ways like the natural environment in Australia before Europeans arrived.

Because there's been no natural predators, you get all kinds of weird . . . things, growing and prospering – breeding – simply because there's nothing there to stop them. To kill and eat them.

And me and a few friends, who are good at our jobs and care about stuff, when we enter these sections we're like rabbits, or. Foxes. Bullfrogs. We can often destroy and unbalance whole ecosystems. But if you're own on your own . . .

Suddenly you're surrounded by all these . . . wombats. Marsupials.

And the reason they can exist like that – live – is even more . . .

In many sections of the Department, the manager's salary relies on how many employees they have at any given time.

So, if someone in the manager's team is deeply incompetent and they try to rectify that the response is nearly always along the lines of:

'If you have issues with my performance then perhaps I should move to another section?'

Which will immediately reduce that manager's wage by two, three per cent – possibly four – because replacing anyone takes months. Years, sometimes. If it even happens.

And they band together in these sections, like proper actual Gypsies, so if one goes, they all do.

And the manager, with a mortgage and school fees and holidays in the Maldives to really really worry about, thinks; 'Fuck it. Fuck it, I'll just. I'll let it go. I will. I'll just, let it go.'

'Just stay.'

'Please.'

'Do what you like.'

But obviously because everyone involved in this process is British, none of this is ever explicitly stated or commented on. It is just. Understood. Happens.

Goes on in the background, without any fuss. Like:

Photosynthesis.

Brownian Motion.

Death.

He smiles.

Pause.

When the Minister said, in 2007 I think – 2006 – that the Department was 'Not fit for purpose', he was entirely right. Completely.

And when you have a manager like Ben, overseeing a section like that, in a Department like that, their outputs. The papers they're producing. Which they spend months, years, drafting, issuing.

He shakes his head.

If each of you now – right? – masturbated into a cup. If we all just stopped everything for a second and just spent ten minutes going at it, furiously, into small plastic cups that I had handed round – men and women, pensioners and children, black and white, brothers and . . . sisters – you (we, together) would literally produce more of worth and value to the UK taxpayer.

And I. I have to clear them.

All of them.

Every, every one.

And what goes out. Is, is my responsibility. And sometimes . . .

Sometimes, you don't really know where to start. Other than, with the spelling.

'There are no Ts, Andrew, in 'miscellaneous'.'

'OK?'

'I think, Glen, you're trying here to spell the word 'tenacious'. Two things, about that, Glen. Firstly, that isn't how you spell 'tenacious', Glen. Secondly, Glen, were you actually after the word 'tenacious', because 'tenacious' doesn't really mean much of anything here, in this context. Does it?'

Those are easier messages to convey, actually. Than:

'Why, Andrew?'

'Why, Glen?'

'Why have you done this?'

Pause.

At first, I tried having a quiet word with Ben.

'Um, yeah.'

'This paper, Ben. It doesn't really. I'm not really sure. What. What it's . . . saying. I don't really understand what . . . questions that this is, is answering. Does it really need to go out this week, do you think?'

The first time I tried this.

He just said:

'Yeah.'

And looked at me.

'OK.'

He nods.

'Right.'

'You're sure?'

'Yep.'

'Right.'

'Right. OK.'

Pause.

And it just . . .

. . .

There's . . . there's a point, where you can't hold it up, on your own. Any section needs at least – at least – three people who really care and know what the fuck they're doing. Otherwise, it's like . . .

. . .

And here – there – it's just . . .

Me.

Pause.

The other thing, about the STD.T – and all sections like it – is that they're always (ironically) celebrating.

I mean you have to bring in drinks or food, or both, every time someone gets promoted, joins, leaves, has a birthday, has a period, gets married, has a baby. All the fucking . . . shit, that people do. And when you have a team of thirty, that means, pretty much every day they're bringing in doughnuts, wine, muffins, Fox's Crunch Creams, Pringles, Doritos, Jammy . . . fucking . . . Dodgers, beer, dips.

Baguettes.

Cheese.

Cider.

Cava.

Endlessly. Endless.

Like some infinite lower-middle-class banquet.

And then.

As well.

Are the . . .

. . .

The nights out.

He shakes his head a little.

Which will start in like a Lloyds or, any Wetherspoons. Somewhere big and faceless, that you can book a table and easily get bar food. Then, later on, you'll end up in some fucking club off Regent Street. Or, Covent Garden. Somewhere they play Eighties music so tedious it could literally make your heart stop. And you find yourself just. Drinking. Proper drinking. Till you wake up. Like it's been some, horrible, desperate dream.

Pause.

So. There was a night out. This time.

We started at a Rat & Parrot, near Victoria. Well actually, we'd started at our desks. Someone had bought in Champagne. Decent Champagne. Bollinger. Which we drank from these little plastic cups.

And it was because Natalie, this huge, weird . . . kangaroo. Had been promoted. Massively, ridiculously, over-promoted. Another cancer in the bloodstream of the Civil Service and we're . . .

Partying, like it's . . .

I mean hang around long enough and someone will give you a fucking . . . office. Or or a huge, massively important project that you can't handle and which if you fail at *completely*, it is somehow – somehow – easier to promote you again, upwards and sideways, to somewhere that you can do less harm.

And so it goes.

That is how. It goes.

Government.

Everywhere.

London. Here. There.

There is no . . . method.

There is no-one in the middle, no Wizard of Oz, pulling all the levers.

There is no . . .

Establishment.

Grand Order.

Fucking . . . lizards.

There is just . . .

Chaos.

Pause.

I mean, there are occasional patterns. Emergent forms. The odd success, here and there. But generally. The suits, the missions statements, the policy drives. All of it.

It's not enough.

It's just . . .

A well-meant lie, told half-well.

He nods.

Pause.

But to say it openly, to question any of it, would, would. Be the end of you. If you pointed out to them all how . . .

They'd set on you. They would.

So:

'Well done Natalie, you really deserve this, yeah.'

Is what I should have said. Is what everyone was saying.

But . . .

When someone asked me, came up to my desk and said: 'Isn't it great news? About Natalie?'

All I could say back, was:

'News.'

And nod.

'News.'

He nods.

In her card, I wrote:

'Natalie. You must be pleased.'

Which I think. I think I got away with.

Pause.

She once asked me, Natalie. She once asked me:

'Why do all the Muslims hate us so much?'

And it was all I could do, to stop myself, from telling her.

Pause.

So I'm at the bar at the Rat & Parrot. I'm already half-cut. After the Bollinger and then starting at the bar with a few Carlsbergs before someone – somewhere – bought Sambucas and I had about three of those. I think. Three. Then. Then there's a tray of vodka shots. That taste. Awful.

I find myself ordering a bottle of Merlot, at the bar. Ask for one glass. Put it on the card.

It tastes . . .

I think it's corked but I can't really be bothered to argue with the poor Polish girl who served me and who has clearly never worked in or near a bar before tonight and hasn't been helped in any way by the Australian bar manager, who I keep hear speaking and who is making me wish I was hard – like a Serbian war criminal, or or or a Yardie – so I could reach over, jump over the bar, grab his head, and . . .

Pause.

I hear him say. The Aussie. 'The thing about English people, it's like they don't even like sex.'

Which is . . .

He shakes his head a little.

I look at him.

But he won't return the, the look.

He's too busy flirting like some . . . With this really young-looking black girl, wearing very tight white jeans.

I've never slept with a black girl.

I'd like to. I would. I mean their skin is so . . .

Well.

Black.

Pause.

I keep staring at the Australian.

But he still won't look at me. He knows.

Then I hear.

Ben.

He's . . .

Next to me, at the bar.

And he asks me if, if I'm going to dance.

Because they're all . . . All of them – the STD.T – are on this little raised floor, opposite us.

Dancing.

Their coats and bags all in a big pile behind them.

I look at Ben. And say:

'I don't want to.'

'Come on mate, don't be such a Lovejoy.'

Pause.

'Killjoy.'

'What?'

'You said Lovejoy. I think you mean Killjoy.'

Pause.

'So . . . ? Are you gonna dance, or what? Natalie really wants you to. I think she quite likes you actually mate.'

And with that, he puts his arm . . .

On and around my shoulder. Pushes me, friendly, towards the dance-floor.

They're playing *Vienna*, by Ultravox.

And the section, the STD.T – they're all there – are . . . they are. Loving it.

Mark, who's an admin support from Bexley Heath, is. Body-popping. Quite well.

Priya, from Croydon, I think, is getting everyone to do a, a Mexican Wave. Around the dance-floor. Even with, with people she doesn't know.

And they're all – they are – everyone is doing it. A Mexican. Fucking. Wave.

And Ben pulls me towards it. This . . . This . . .

. . .

So yes.

I am.

I am a Lovejoy.

I swig from the Merlot, the bottle, pushing back at Ben –
not friendly – trying to stop before we get there because if I
physically step onto the dance-floor, there's no . . . there's
no coming back.

I force Ben away, pretty hard, and he says:

'Easy mate.'

I wipe Merlot from my face. It's down on my neck, shirt.

Red.

I'm covered in medium-priced wine.

I say: 'Sorry.'

'Sorry mate.'

And he says:

'Are you OK?'

He seems to mean it.

Pause.

'No.'

I say.

'No, I'm not.'

'Right. Do you need a taxi then or something?'

Do I need a taxi?

In many ways, I do, yeah.

I mean, it could speed off the road, through, into the bar, roll over several times, explode in a horrific ball of flames and take me and all of them out.

Yeah.

But it won't.

It never does.

Pause.

Though.

There must have be someone, somewhere, high in one of the Twin Towers.

Someone like me.

Who had been. Broken. Over time.

Some frustrated New Yorker – industrious, Jewish, in the middle of drinking their first coffee of the morning – who saw that first plane coming. Saw it through the window. Approaching.

Like no other plane ever had. At that. Odd angle.

The angle of, of rage.

Of.

Revenge.

And knew.

Immediately.

Knew exactly what was happening.

Why.

And he or she will have dropped their coffee onto the ground, broken into the broadest of smiles. And thought:

'Yes.'

'At last.'

Pause.

And as it got nearer.

As they started to feel the heat from the engines.

The gathering noise.

'Yes.'

'Come.'

'Take me.'

The building starting to shake.

'Take us. Take all of us.'

'Burn every one.'

'Thank you.'

'Yes.'

Pause.

Ben has his hand on my shoulder.

I'm leaning over to one side.

He's saying:

'You could maybe do with going home mate, I reckon. Do you want me to sort out a taxi for you?'

Doing his . . . this voice. Like we're . . .

But I tell him. I ask him.

'I've got some coke.'

'What?'

'I've got some coke. Would you like some coke?'

And he's all:

'I'm not sure that's a good idea mate, you're a bit . . . '

But I . . .

I insist.

'No, no it will clear my head. Help me get home OK. Honestly. Always works. Always.'

'You're sure?'

'Yeah.'

He nods.

Yeah.

And so he half-carries me into the men's toilets.

We go into a cubicle. Together.

He locks the door.

And we stand.

For a while.

Pause.

'So . . . so where is it?'

'What?'

'The coke mate. Is it in a wrap or something?'

I smile at him. Fixed.

'I haven't. I haven't got any.'

'Right.'

And there is a . . .

A silence.

Silence.

'So what are we . . . doing here, mate?'

And I say.

'Ben.'

'Now.'

'Now.'

'Listen to me.'

'You. You are bad at your job.'

He nods.

'Awful.'

'You are . . . '

'Worse than . . . '

'Stupid. Actually stupid. You're well-educated, you have a
PhD, I know that, but you're . . . '

' . . . '

'Something inside you has . . . '

'I mean, you don't understand *people*, you don't understand . . .
work. You don't understand the concept of work in its
broadest terms. You don't know how *people work*.'

'If there was any justice – actual fucking justice – you would
be fired. And then, physically beaten.'

'I mean . . . '

'Working with you, for you, has been the single worst
experience. Of my life. Of my. Whole life.'

'You're . . . '

'A posh. Full-on. Spastic. In a pinstripe.'

'Who seems to think that he . . . that he matters.'

'But he doesn't.'

'You don't.'

'All that you do.'

'The only way, that you matter.'

'Is that you suck.'

'Skill.'

'Time.'

'Money.'

'Food.'

'Oxygen.'

'Hope.'

'Love.'

'From me. And all the other people.'

'In the world.'

'You.'

He nods.

'Yeah.'

'And I, I definitely don't have any coke.'

'That.'

'That, was a lie.'

Silence.

'Dave.'

That's all he says.

Dave.

My name.

He looks at me for a bit. Can tell that I mean it. That I mean all of it.

His head wavers slightly and then. He looks down.

Mumbles to himself. Again.

Just:

'Dave.'

Like I've . . .

And then he, he goes.

He nods.

Pause.

By the time I get outside, out into the bar, he's got his coat on, picked up his man-bag and he's already heading out onto the street.

I clatter through the bar and I can see that's everyone's stopped dancing. The STD.T. They're all looking in the direction, of where Ben has gone. There's obviously . . . been a scene. And now they're . . . they're all looking at me.

But I keep going.

Push the door. Get outside.

Fresh air's suddenly . . .

And I see Ben getting into a black cab and I shout after him but it pulls past and off.

He doesn't hear, see me.

But I . . .

I see him.

And he's . . .

He's . . .

Yeah.

He's crying.

Quietly.

He's got his bag, on his lap, which he's holding. And he's . . .

And the taxi goes. Gone.

Pause.

I take a swig from the bottle of Merlot.

Breathe.

Watch.

Traffic.

Remember, the last person that I made cry.

Lauren.

This is – must be – four, four years ago. We went out for ten months and I thought that I didn't love her. I didn't think that I . . .

And I . . .

Rather than let it . . .

. . .

Finished it.

And she. Cried. When I told her.

She was sat on her bed and she said:

'But I think you're lovely.'

Which was so . . .

Simple.

Honest.

Such a . . .

To say that.

To me.

Pause.

Take another swig. Watch more traffic. Mainly taxis. The odd. Cyclist.

Pause.

Now. I can't go back in but I really don't want to go home.

Home is a flat-share in Finsbury Park.

Two girls, they work in marketing. A boy, recruitment consultant. And me.

And every single day I get up at least half an hour before they do, so that I don't have to travel in on the tube with them.

They're not. Monsters. I just can't talk in the morning, I'm not . . . switched on yet.

But then, I can barely do it in the evenings. Weekends.

They're always watching *Dexter*. They have the box-set. Series 1. Whatever time I seem to come in, they're always watching. Series 1 of fucking. *Dexter*.

He shakes his head.

I can't go home.

I can't.

So I just . . .

Start to . . . to walk.

Buy a small bottle of Smirnoff at an Off Licence, pour it into the wine bottle. Shake it up.

Tastes.

Good.

Really, really quite good. And things go a little . . . hazy.

I thought. Now I thought, I'd closed my eyes just for a second but when, when I open them. I'm leaning against a building.

Yeah.

I look up and it's. It's the House of Lords.

Beautiful, really.

High. Stone.

Then I wander round. Parliament Square. Look at the statues. Of Cromwell. Churchill.

Mandela.

Pause.

And I make a decision.

I'm going to see Ben.

Tonight.

And in preparation for the walk I go to this little Tesco next to Westminster tube and I buy four cans of Carlsberg, a packet of Cheese and Onion Hula Hoops and some Minstrels.

And I just.

Start.

Off. Into the night.

First, over Westminster Bridge. Then, down by the river. Past St Thomas, the hospital. Parliament on the other side of the water now.

And after some weird office buildings, petrol station, I get to the gay bars of Vauxhall. Fire. Sweat. Area.

Then, under a bridge and through this little Portugese district.

There's tapas.

Bars.

The odd disco.

Lots of people smoking outside.

Women with lovely Mediterranean curves and slightly rough faces.

I'm heading towards Clapham – South London – because I know that's on the way. The way to Ben.

But I'm not there yet. I'm going up this road, near where I used to live. Which gets me to Stockwell.

And I stop for a while, look at the shrine, to Jean Charles De Menezes. The guy who got. And I wonder, if I'd have shot him. If I'd been . . .

. . .

And I come to the conclusion that yeah, I probably would. I'm not very well co-ordinated. I'm a coward. I was terrible at paintball. I'd just have panicked and . . .

Bang.

Pause.

Just past the station, I see Byron.

And you won't know this but Byron is a black Rastafarian alcoholic midget, who roams Stockwell and Vauxhall, nearly always carrying a little plastic bag, which is full of super strength lager. Yeah, I don't think he's had a good life.

And Byron is sat on a bench, being talked to by this girl. Young. White. Middle-class. Nearly pretty. And all I can think is:

What a patronising. Stupid. Bitch.

She probably thinks that she's . . . somehow . . . helping him, by . . . Talking.

But she's not.

She's a rubber-necker. Do-good. Pussy. Bullshit.

And I walk on.

Angry now.

Speed up.

A bit coz I'm mad but also because it's Stockwell and really quite scary.

I'd forgotten that.

And after what seems like eight years of horrible estates on my right and lovely Victorian houses on my left, I get to Clapham.

Clapham High Street.

It's . . .

. . .

It's like.

Every vaguely posh graduate that you ever thought was the biggest prick you'd ever met in your life and they've all had a meeting – an AGM – and decided to live in the same area.

They're everywhere. Swarming around like . . .

I pass one bar, called The Railway, and there's a party of friends sat outside on these wooden benches. About ten of them.

And every single one of them is wearing . . . silver or gold . . . accessories, sunglasses, scarves, pork-pie hats, ironic moustaches, something that says:

'Hey!'

'Yeah!'

'Look at me!'

'God yeah!'

I mean, there's not a single moment of doubt between them.

Of honour. Decency.

And without really thinking about it, I throw an unopened can of Carlsberg at them and it hits this blonde girl sat on the end.

Fairly hard. On the head.

Knocks her over. Her hair sort of flicks up as she . . . goes
. . . down.

It doesn't draw blood or anything, she's conscious I think
but . . .

There follows a bit of a. Commotion.

During which I . . . I run.

I run away.

He nods.

Pause.

I stop once I know I'm OK. Safe. Can't hear anyone chasing
me, I'm sweating like a . . .

On a back-street. Residential. Quiet.

And I can't really get my breath yet. So I, I sit down on the
pavement, open another lager. My last.

Pause.

I wake up again. This time I'm, I'm in a field.

It's proper dark – black – and all I can see are trees and
grass in silhouette.

Fucking . . .

Everywhere.

. . .

I'm in a dark field.

The country.

. . .

But then I, I focus a bit. Make myself focus. Get my
bearings. It's OK, it's, it's OK . . . it's, it's just the Common.

I'm sat on the Common. Clapham Common. I've had a kip on the Common. It's fine. It's OK. It's . . . it's alright.

He nods a little.

I get up.

Heads towards the traffic.

Stumble. Retch.

Get to the road.

There's the odd taxi. Lorry.

I follow it. The road. To my right. Like an adventurer or tribesman would with a river and when I do get to the end, I cross another road and there is a sea of sorts, of. Beautiful residential housing.

I stand, and look. Can see neat little balconies. Conservatories. Actual chandeliers.

The odd person has left the light on.

The bastards.

And I imagine all the people – rich, white people, who wear elegant simple clothes and know how to cook things from scratch with entirely fresh ingredients – who live in them. And I wonder where they. Where do they educate their children.

I'm from a provincial town. Where most people are educated in comprehensives. Like I was. But not these people. They would never let their . . .

And I don't know what public, private schools are like in London: you never see them.

And I imagine for a second that they're hidden underneath – directly underneath – all the shitty schools that the black and Asian and eastern European children go to and that you do see fucking . . . everywhere. So whilst all these poor kids are barely getting an education, doing their best to avoid being stabbed, in the basements beneath their feet. Jocasta and Jack and Chloe are being told, very firmly:

'You. You are the best.'

'You are the absolute best. Always remember that.'

'The children above you. They know nothing. They are ethnically, culturally, inferior. You. You are the future. You are the past. You are . . . '

'The fucking . . . '

'All.'

And I if I ever have children. I want them. In the basement. Being told that.

Because no-one . . .

No-one ever told me.

So my children – if I ever have them – will.

They will be told.

I keep going.

Suddenly, I'm being sick outside a Waterstones near Clapham Junction.

Anger of the Gods-style. Pretty much the entire entrance to Waterstones is veneered in bits of, of me. Including a Minstrel that I must have swallowed whole.

I get a very dirty look from a group of attractive young slags walking past but I couldn't give less of a . . . Stare all you like, I'm still going to look at your legs, tits and arseholes. In that order.

Which I may have said out loud.

I'm sick again and one of the girls screams:

'Oh my God that is fucking sick!'

Well. Yes. Yes it is.

I'm bent over but I give her a thumbs up above my head and wipe some away with the back of my hand. Smile.

Which leaves her:

Aroused, no doubt.

He smiles.

Horrendously, with the extra clear-headedness from having thrown up, I find the wherewithal to go into a dodgy newsagent and despite the fact that it's half one in the morning, buy a bottle of Stowell's Chenin Blanc. Six ninety-nine.

Screw top.

Goes down a treat. Fills me . . . fills me . . . with . . .

Pause.

I'm. I'm at a McDonald's counter. Demanding a burger.

They're saying it's breakfast-only but I desperately need – demand – a burger.

I lose my temper a bit.

'I want a fucking burger mate.'

And I notice – weirdly – it's starting to get light, outside.

'I want a fucking . . . Quarterpounder meal. No, Big Mac. Big Mac. Big fucking. Mac.'

'We're only doing breakfasts.'

'*What?*'

So I get a muffin. And, and an orange juice.

Then, for a while I think I know where I'm going – I pass a garden centre that looks familiar and a bridge – but . . .

Soon – somehow – I'm back at the same McDonald's. And it's the same guy serving me. He looks. Hispanic. Maybe Syrian. Arab. Something.

I demand, again, I demand a burger.

But I get another . . .

McMuffin.

Move on.

Still quite hungry.

Pause.

It's miles.

Through Battersea, I'm in Battersea, which is actually alright. Not as a place but for where I'm going. To Ben. It means I'm heading in the right direction.

Though I'm glad I'm only passing through because it's . . .

It's so . . .

They're so many estates, tower blocks – I . . .

There's so many I have to force myself not to think about all the people – kids – who live there.

These miles of . . .

Endless . . .

Being born into that.

He shakes his head a little.

I keep walking. Away from them and I think, now, I'm, I'm on Garratt Lane. There are pubs that serve Thai food. Shops. Still the odd person around. I see three different people walking dogs. All, very small, tiny dogs.

It's light.

Looks. Lighter.

Yellow.

Some clouds.

I keep going. Trying to . . .

Get towards Earlsfield train station and here is where I need to start veering right.

And – after a little bit, back to nice residential – I get to the park.

Wimbledon Park. Near to where they play all the lovely tennis.

It's closed.

But I, I climb over the fence.

Easy.

And it's so.

Quiet.

Calm.

Green.

I'm the only person in the whole park.

I walk over the grass, slowly, towards the water, the, this lake on the other side.

And when I get there.

There are swans.

Asleep.

On a little dock.

And I watch them.

Breathing.

It's so . . .

. . .

Look out at the water.

Pause.

When I die, I'd like to drown. Not in the sea. In Scotland.
In a loch. In dark and deep fresh-water and my body to be
found days later by a young professional couple pushing a
buggy with a disabled – severely disfigured – child in it.
Yeah.

I keep . . .

Through the park. Pass tennis courts. Swings. Playground.

I climb another fence, on the other side. Pavement.

I'm near.

Ben.

Pause.

My brother married into money, if you can believe that. She's
big in . . . something financial and near completely evil. It
might even be a, a Hedge Fund. She's a Fat Cat, essentially.

Nice though. Very giving. Funny.

I head on.

Past Wimbledon Park Station.

Past all the side-streets.

Really posh, really very nice.

And then.

There.

My brother's house.

Which he didn't pay a fucking penny for.

Three floors. A basement. Garden. Georgian.

I stand outside. Look at all the . . . the bricks. The lovely,
lovely bricks.

Walk down the path at the side of the house. Open the gate
and walk into the back garden.

I'd kill to have a garden.

It's light.

The sky is . . .

Orange.

Blue.

I stand on the grass.

And there he is.

Ben.

Through the conservatory doors, I can see him. Playing Guitar Hero on his Wii. Concentrating. He always gets up very early, before school, to play. I knew that but . . . to see him.

I walk to the doors.

Knock on the glass.

Ben looks up, gets the key from the mantel piece, opens the door and asks me:

'What are you doing here, Uncle David?'

'Saying . . . hello.'

'Hello.'

He looks up at me. Smiles, and let's me in. Next thing he says:

'Would you like to play Guitar Hero?'

He nods.

'Thank you Ben. That would be . . . '

But I can't really work it out, it's horribly difficult. You have to press buttons which relate to notes – at exactly the right time – which makes the music on the screen play and you get points, or . . . He shows me how, he's very patient with me. But my co-ordination is . . .

After a bit, I just let him play, sit back and watch.

He's. Incredible. It really is a skill in its own right. Entirely pointless – entirely – but . . .

What isn't?

Pause.

Whilst he's focussing on the game, I ask him:

'What's your school like, Ben? It's private, isn't it?'

'Yeah.'

'Is it . . . is it underground?'

'No.'

He nods.

'OK.'

Pause.

And the weirdest thing about Guitar Hero is that all the music, is Eighties. Terrible Eighties. Like. Mega Death. The Scorpions. Def Leppard.

And the kids.

Kids now.

They love it.

I mean, Ben. Ben is always saying that his favourite band. Is – are – The Scorpions. And his favourite song. Of all time. Of all the music made by any human throughout history. Is *Wind of Change*. That awful, awful tune with the whistling and the . . .

An awful song.

But Ben puts down the controller and says:

'Shall we dance to The Scorpions?'

Pause.

'What?'

'Shall we dance to The Scorpions?'

Pause.

And I say:

'OK.'

I'd forgotten.

Ben loves to dance. His favourite television programme is *Strictly Come Dancing*. He's got a massive crush on Alesha Dixon. Fair enough.

He nods.

So he puts on *Wind of Change*, on this little stereo behind us.

Pause.

And we dance.

He stands on my feet.

I lead, obviously.

He looks up at me.

As we dance.

And says:

'Uncle David, is this good music?'

And I say:

Pause.

'Yes.'

'Yes, this is good music.'

Pause.

'Is it, is it the best song of all time, do ya think?'

OK.

A long pause.

'Yes Ben, this is the best song of all time.'

And he smiles.

We dance.

Pause.

Then I ask him:

'Am I . . . ? Ben. Listen to me, would you – honestly, tell me, honestly, please – do you think that I'm going . . . am I'm gonna be . . . alright?'

I ask.

And he says:

'How do you mean?'

And I say:

'With everything. My life. Will it all work out? Honestly?'

Pause.

And Benjamin looks up at me.

Shrugs, just shrugs. And says:

'I don't know.'

'I don't know.'

Pause.

And we dance.

We dance around the conservatory.

Methuen Drama Student Editions

Jean Anouilh *Antigone* • John Arden *Serjeant Musgrave's Dance*
Alan Ayckbourn *Confusions* • Aphra Behn *The Rover* • Edward Bond
Lear • *Saved* • Bertolt Brecht *The Caucasian Chalk Circle* • *Fear and
Misery in the Third Reich* • *The Good Person of Szechwan* • *Life of Galileo* •
Mother Courage and her Children• *The Resistible Rise of Arturo Ui* • *The
Threepenny Opera* • Anton Chekhov *The Cherry Orchard* • *The Seagull* •
Three Sisters • *Uncle Vanya* • Caryl Churchill *Serious Money* • *Top Girls*
• Shelagh Delaney *A Taste of Honey* • Euripides *Elektra* • *Medea*•
Dario Fo *Accidental Death of an Anarchist* • Michael Frayn *Copenhagen*
• John Galsworthy *Strife* • Nikolai Gogol *The Government Inspector* •
Robert Holman *Across Oka* • Henrik Ibsen *A Doll's House* • *Ghosts*•
Hedda Gabler • Charlotte Keatley *My Mother Said I Never Should* •
Bernard Kops *Dreams of Anne Frank* • Federico García Lorca *Blood
Wedding* • *Doña Rosita the Spinster* (bilingual edition) •*The House of
Bernarda Alba* • (bilingual edition) • *Yerma* (bilingual edition) • David
Mamet *Glengarry Glen Ross* • *Oleanna* • Patrick Marber *Closer* • John
Marston *Malcontent* • Martin McDonagh *The Lieutenant of Inishmore* •
Joe Orton *Loot* • Luigi Pirandello *Six Characters in Search of an Author*
• Mark Ravenhill *Shopping and F***ing* • Willy Russell *Blood Brothers*
• *Educating Rita* • Sophocles *Antigone* • *Oedipus the King* • Wole
Soyinka *Death and the King's Horseman* • Shelagh Stephenson *The
Memory of Water* • August Strindberg *Miss Julie* • J. M. Synge *The
Playboy of the Western World* • Theatre Workshop *Oh What a Lovely
War* Timberlake Wertenbaker *Our Country's Good* • Arnold Wesker
The Merchant • Oscar Wilde *The Importance of Being Earnest* •
Tennessee Williams *A Streetcar Named Desire* • *The Glass Menagerie*

Methuen Drama Modern Plays

include work by

Edward Albee
Jean Anouilh
John Arden
Margaretta D'Arcy
Peter Barnes
Sebastian Barry
Brendan Behan
Dermot Bolger
Edward Bond
Bertolt Brecht
Howard Brenton
Anthony Burgess
Simon Burke
Jim Cartwright
Caryl Churchill
Complicite
Noël Coward
Lucinda Coxon
Sarah Daniels
Nick Darke
Nick Dear
Shelagh Delaney
David Edgar
David Eldridge
Dario Fo
Michael Frayn
John Godber
Paul Godfrey
David Greig
John Guare
Peter Handke
David Harrower
Jonathan Harvey
Iain Heggie
Declan Hughes
Terry Johnson
Sarah Kane
Charlotte Keatley
Barrie Keeffe

Howard Korder
Robert Lepage
Doug Lucie
Martin McDonagh
John McGrath
Terrence McNally
David Mamet
Patrick Marber
Arthur Miller
Mtwa, Ngema & Simon
Tom Murphy
Phyllis Nagy
Peter Nichols
Sean O'Brien
Joseph O'Connor
Joe Orton
Louise Page
Joe Penhall
Luigi Pirandello
Stephen Poliakoff
Franca Rame
Mark Ravenhill
Philip Ridley
Reginald Rose
Willy Russell
Jean-Paul Sartre
Sam Shepard
Wole Soyinka
Simon Stephens
Shelagh Stephenson
Peter Straughan
C. P. Taylor
Theatre Workshop
Sue Townsend
Judy Upton
Timberlake Wertenbaker
Roy Williams
Snoo Wilson
Victoria Wood

Methuen Drama Modern Classics

Jean Anouilh *Antigone* • Brendan Behan *The Hostage* • Robert Bolt *A Man for All Seasons* • Edward Bond *Saved* • Bertolt Brecht *The Caucasian Chalk Circle* • *Fear and Misery in the Third Reich* • *The Good Person of Szechwan* • *Life of Galileo* • *The Messingkauf Dialogues* • *Mother Courage and Her Children* • *Mr Puntila and His Man Matti* • *The Resistible Rise of Arturo Ui* • *Rise and Fall of the City of Mahagonny* • *The Threepenny Opera* • Jim Cartwright *Road* • *Two & Bed* • Caryl Churchill *Serious Money* • *Top Girls* • Noël Coward *Blithe Spirit* • *Hay Fever* • *Present Laughter* • *Private Lives* • *The Vortex* • Shelagh Delaney *A Taste of Honey* • Dario Fo *Accidental Death of an Anarchist* • Michael Frayn *Copenhagen* • Lorraine Hansberry *A Raisin in the Sun* • Jonathan Harvey *Beautiful Thing* • David Mamet *Glengarry Glen Ross* • *Oleanna* • *Speed-the-Plow* • Patrick Marber *Closer* • *Dealer's Choice* • Arthur Miller *Broken Glass* • Percy Mtwa, Mbongeni Ngema, Barney Simon *Woza Albert!* • Joe Orton *Entertaining Mr Sloane* • *Loot* • *What the Butler Saw* • Mark Ravenhill *Shopping and F***ing* • Willy Russell *Blood Brothers* • *Educating Rita* • *Stags and Hens* • *Our Day Out* • Jean-Paul Sartre *Crime Passionnel* • Wole Soyinka • *Death and the King's Horseman* • Theatre Workshop *Oh, What a Lovely War* • Frank Wedekind • *Spring Awakening* • Timberlake Wertenbaker *Our Country's Good*

Methuen Drama Contemporary Dramatists

include

John Arden (two volumes)
Arden & D'Arcy
Peter Barnes (three volumes)
Sebastian Barry
Dermot Bolger
Edward Bond (eight volumes)
Howard Brenton
  (two volumes)
Richard Cameron
Jim Cartwright
Caryl Churchill (two volumes)
Sarah Daniels (two volumes)
Nick Darke
David Edgar (three volumes)
David Eldridge
Ben Elton
Dario Fo (two volumes)
Michael Frayn (three volumes)
David Greig
John Godber (four volumes)
Paul Godfrey
John Guare
Lee Hall (two volumes)
Peter Handke
Jonathan Harvey
  (two volumes)
Declan Hughes
Terry Johnson (three volumes)
Sarah Kane
Barrie Keeffe
Bernard-Marie Koltès
  (two volumes)
Franz Xaver Kroetz
David Lan
Bryony Lavery
Deborah Levy
Doug Lucie

David Mamet (four volumes)
Martin McDonagh
Duncan McLean
Anthony Minghella
  (two volumes)
Tom Murphy (six volumes)
Phyllis Nagy
Anthony Neilsen (two volumes)
Philip Osment
Gary Owen
Louise Page
Stewart Parker (two volumes)
Joe Penhall (two volumes)
Stephen Poliakoff
  (three volumes)
David Rabe (two volumes)
Mark Ravenhill (two volumes)
Christina Reid
Philip Ridley
Willy Russell
Eric-Emmanuel Schmitt
Ntozake Shange
Sam Shepard (two volumes)
Wole Soyinka (two volumes)
Simon Stephens (two volumes)
Shelagh Stephenson
David Storey (three volumes)
Sue Townsend
Judy Upton
Michel Vinaver
  (two volumes)
Arnold Wesker (two volumes)
Michael Wilcox
Roy Williams (three volumes)
Snoo Wilson (two volumes)
David Wood (two volumes)
Victoria Wood

Methuen Drama Classical Greek Dramatists

Aeschylus Plays: One
(Persians, Seven Against Thebes, Suppliants,
Prometheus Bound)

Aeschylus Plays: Two
(Oresteia: Agamemnon, Libation-Bearers, Eumenides)

Aristophanes Plays: One
(Acharnians, Knights, Peace, Lysistrata)

Aristophanes Plays: Two
(Wasps, Clouds, Birds, Festival Time, Frogs)

Aristophanes & Menander: New Comedy
(Women in Power, Wealth, The Malcontent,
The Woman from Samos)

Euripides Plays: One
(Medea, The Phoenician Women, Bacchae)

Euripides Plays: Two
(Hecuba, The Women of Troy, Iphigeneia at Aulis,
Cyclops)

Euripides Plays: Three
(Alkestis, Helen, Ion)

Euripides Plays: Four
(Elektra, Orestes, Iphigeneia in Tauris)

Euripides Plays: Five
(Andromache, Herakles' Children, Herakles)

Euripides Plays: Six
(Hippolytos, Suppliants, Rhesos)

Sophocles Plays: One
(Oedipus the King, Oedipus at Colonus, Antigone)

Sophocles Plays: Two
(Ajax, Women of Trachis, Electra, Philoctetes)